My Journey

With Addiction

Versey A. Williams

A Christian Bible Studies Publication
www.ChristianStudies7.com

ISBN 0-9763357-1-9

Printed in the United States of America
Color House Graphics
Grand Rapids, MI

This has not been easy.

*Thank you to the people who
encouraged me to tell my story.*

*Many knew, others suspected.
A few tried to warn me.*

*It is time to face my pain.
It is time to mourn.*

*They prayed with me,
they stayed with me in my pain.*

*They encouraged me.
They helped me trust again.*

*They are my Colleague Group
and our Mentor.
They helped me get past my shame.*

*My midwife, the Director of the Doctorate of
Ministry Program. He encouraged me to write.*

*The Sisterhood, they encircled and held me.
I am no longer alone, and*

*My shepherd, his wife and my church family.
They kept me afloat when I began to sink again.*

*These are they whom God gave me.
They helped me become whole again.*

The Table of Contents

The Introduction

Enroute to Phoenix, a lady was nice enough to share her newspaper with me. The headlines read, "Seven year old girl brings $1,000.00 worth of crack to school. Mother under investigation." No doubt dad is probably not present or at least not keeping tabs on his baby girl. I can only imagine what life is like at home for her. Actually, I don't have to imagine. I know what life is like living with crack-cocaine.

When crack finally revealed itself to me, it was not a pretty picture. It had made no pretenses. We had lived together many years. I knew it well. It ruled my home. It was mysterious, but it wasn't distant. I felt its presence. It often threw me to my knees. It let me know that it would sacrifice anything for itself. Crack is vicious, evil personified. It is never a guest, it owns its victims. Crack doesn't just lie around. It must be the center of attention. It doesn't tarry and never runs out of energy. It's creative survival skill pushes it's victims beyond capacity and it knows no limits. There is nothing that crack would not do for itself.

Crack-cocaine almost destroyed my life. It continues to haunt me. I can sometimes hear it's whisper. It reminds me of what it took from me. I did not want to face it again. My memories wouldn't leave me alone. They reminded me of the suffering and humiliation. I sometimes hurt as though it was just yesterday. It never apologized to me. It never cared about my wounded soul. I keep trying to make some sense of it all. Sometimes the tears still flow. The tears remind me of the battle that took place in my house. I did not have a home until crack left the premises. Once I learned its name, we could not share the same house. My house longed to be a home but crack would have no part in a home. It only cared about itself. Crack and I could no longer co-exist. It had proved itself lethal. It destroyed my marriage and it was trying to destroy me.

Pain ceases to be suffering where there is meaning and purpose. I pray that my journey will help someone pick up his or her broken pieces and live again. Rebuilding my life has been the most difficult thing I have ever had to do. My dreams were shattered. Crack never cared about my future. It only cared about itself. With the help of God and friends, life is well worth living again. For years, I thought I would never stop hurting. I tried to dull the pain. I lied. I covered. I thought myself above the abuse. Perhaps if I pretended, it would go away. I was too proud to tell. Living a lie was easier than facing the truth. The pain continues to follow me. I am now facing my painful memories, the betrayal, and the abuse. Each day I am growing stronger. This is my journey with addiction.

My Transformation

Fifty is a very good year. August 14, 2004 was a very good day. I like being 50. I should have been 50 first. My children, who am I kidding? My daughter hosted a lovely outdoor dinner for me. My sons, as usual, showed up. My oldest son reminds me that his wife takes up his slack. She does a remarkable job. The past 49 years have been an interesting journey. Was the glass half empty or half full? Has my life been problematic or extraordinary? Extraordinarily problematic sounds good. I had lunch with Mom yesterday, it was pleasant. I stopped by Dad's on the way home. My visits with them are always nice. It hasn't always been this way. They are much different now than I remember them as a child. They were always fighting. I don't remember a civil word between my parents when I was a child.

After 49 years, my parents struck up this friendship. Mother had taken ill a year ago. She had major surgery in January. God really gave her a miracle. Dad helped us care for her. They were actually parents or showed some semblance of what parents could be. Wow, at first I did not like it. I resented them for getting along. How dare they be kind to one another and show mutual concern for me now. I needed parents then, not now.

Can I handle this? I worked hard to overcome their absenteeism. Now I learn they were capable of being considerate to one another? They were even protective of one another! "Teny, have you checked on your mother?" "Teny, have you checked on your father?" They double-teamed me. The nerve of them. Where was my protection when we were left at home with a very angry brother? Now is not the time to reform. I needed parents then! I've come to accept my life. I actually appreciate my parents. I know they had their own obstacles to overcome. They too are products of their parents, their environment and history. I am an adult. I understand these things. Paul wasn't lying when he said that all things work together for the good of those of us who love the Lord and are called according to his purpose. (Romans 8:28). The words of God transformed my ridiculous life. Internalizing the complexities of my parents' lives left little room for dignity and self worth. Neither were afforded or given me. Both have come at a very high price. In 1984, while attending a seminar, the transformation began. Unbeknown to me, my instructor would be the catalyst to a better life. He asked too many questions. I wasn't the friendliest person then. Certainly, my pleasing personality has evolved over these many years. I ignored him and finally sought to avoid him. One evening, trying to pass his dormitory without his interference, he interrupted me (again). Responding to my rudeness, he replied, "God must not love you." Silly man, of course God loves me! His accusation and my biblical response went on a few minutes longer. I asked why he would say such foolishness. Finally he said, "If God loved you he would not have let your parents hurt you." Made sense on the surface. Yet, I know that God loves me because he died for me. "True", my parents left much to be desired by me. Also true is that God's love is able to withstand the fallout of my problematic life. Bingo! Out of the depths of my soul, I realized that I could have a better life. It was up to me. For the first time, I thought there may be a possibility they did the best they could or at least their neglect would no longer hold me inferior to the world.

   As God would have it, my roommate did not show up that night. I knelt by my bed and asked God to forgive me for a few things. I wanted to talk to Daddy. I hadn't spoken to him in many years. Daddy left home when I was about 13 years old. Mother told me that he left for many reasons – one being my fault. I tried to repair the damage but I just couldn't. He never came back home. For the next 19 years, I would try to win Daddy's approval and love. I had good grades, worked, paid my bills, and was recognized for many civic achievements. I remember receiving the Business Woman of the Year Award in 1984. It was great. I received a standing ovation. I went immediately to show Daddy. He wasn't impressed at all. I can't remember what happened to that plaque. Within one hour, it had lost its meaning.

   My parents' union had already placed a substantial dent in my self-esteem. The years that followed their divorce were challenging. Life after Daddy left home became even more difficult. My mother's frequent absences eventually made Daddy take my sister to live with him and my new step-mother. Home on the ranch became more shameful. Mother's drinking increased along with the lifestyle that accompanies such social activity. If we had been living in this day and time, my sister and I probably would have been placed in foster care. Our house would have been condemned.

I managed to graduate from high school in 1972 with good grades but little preparation for my future. While sitting in Baccalaureate, I heard the word *college*. No one had ever mentioned it to me before. I wanted to go there. I had been working since my freshman year. Finances were not available to me so I had to work and support myself. There didn't seem room for college. By my senior year, I had too much responsibility not to work.

In a strange kind of way, my children gave me some stability. I feel such delight when I look at my only daughter. Though she (and her brothers) bore the brunt of my immaturity, with the help of the Lord, I was able to shape her into a beautiful rose. My, how she has blossomed. My innocence was stolen from me. It is nice to have a glimpse of what life should have been like for me. Ill prepared to become a parent complicated matters. I bought our first home when I was 19. Finally, I had a home! It was lovely. I had a home I could be proud of. We moved in with a few boxes and some furniture. I had no housekeeping skills but I took pride in our new home. I had no concept of what a real family looked like or how a real family behaved. Nonetheless, I finally had a home to be proud of and my children would always have a place they could call home.

Shame, humiliation, and loneliness best describe my life well into adulthood. The silver lining contained my wonderful paternal grandparents and my Pa Pa. Let me introduce you to my Pa Pa. He was my paternal great-grandfather. A wonderful man. I still remember his dark frame. He was good to me. He hugged me and spent time with me. He actually gave me whiskey and I got sick. Finally the doctors told Daddy I was a little drunk! Just kidding. I am told that when Pa Pa (and my) secret was discovered, Pa Pa was sorry for his misdoing. I don't think I got drunk after that. We used to sit on the heat register and fall asleep. I still have the scar from being burned when I was a little girl! It is a good scar! Pa Pa died. It was April 16, 1965. I was 10 years old. I remember him lying in the reddish box. He wouldn't get up. I kept calling him but he was sleep. I waited at the top of the steps many nights before I went to bed. I cried and cried. I called him but he did not come home. He always had time for me. I missed Pa Pa. We did not see much of Miss Lula after Pa Pa died. Miss Lula Jones was Pa Pa's lady friend. I missed her too. She always had time for me. We would sleep with her. Pa Pa slept in the chair or somewhere most of the time since it would be my sister and me in the bed with Miss. Lula. She always wore a bonnet on her hair. She always plaited our hair. Even now when I pass by their street, I can imagine us all sitting on the stone stoop.

The silver lining was full of goodness. I had two wonderful paternal grandparents. My Dad's mother and father each remarried. Grandma Bea was my father's mother. She and Schach were full of life. They let us dance to Chuck Berry. My sister and I twisted and shouted every chance we could! They always had orange sherbet and all kinds of treats for us. Their refrigerator freezer opened from the bottom. I always thought that was a bit weird. They were both very special to me. Schach especially encouraged me every chance he could. We would sit for hours and discuss whatever problem I had. He also celebrated my accomplishments. Grandma Bea was introverted. She was a quiet presence. Sometimes I forget she is dead. I buried them both. I did not think the earth could hold my tears. I loved my grandparents. Grandma Bea died in August 1993. Schach died in December 1985.

Where do I begin with Granddaddy (my Dad's father) and Lucille? They were a pair! Their fussing was poetic. It had a certain rhythm to it. "Lucille." "What do you want Lonzo?" And the argument was on. We spent lots of time with them too. My baby cousin, Rance, also lived with them. Rance could play an organ! We (actually he) would play and I would preach. We mocked church folks. It seemed that Granddaddy's religion included church every waking hour of the day! There was just as much fussing at church as there was in their home. I liked to go to church with them. We got gum from the ladies and they thought we were so cute. They would get happy and scare us to death.

Lucille's house was neat all of the time. She had starched doilies on the coffee and end tables. Granddaddy liked nice things and they lived quite well. Fancy, fancy, fancy, as long as I could remember. There was always an aroma coming from my grandmother's kitchen. Her homemade biscuits were good. In fact, her everything was good. We all ate together at the kitchen table. It seemed like

Granddaddy prayed forever but eventually we did eat.

In the last few years of his life he was pretty mean to her. I used to take up for her when he was impolite to her in front of me. Granddaddy told me he was afraid to die. One day I told him that he should be scared since he was on his way to hell. It shocked him. It was actually kind of funny. I told him that he could not see God if he did not learn how to love his wife. I used to read the Bible to Granddaddy and pray with him when he was sick. Lucille stayed by his side until he died in April 1987. My grandma wanted me to say encouraging words about him at the funeral. At that time the Baptist people did not believe in women preachers or women in the pulpit. The pastor would not allow me in the pulpit. I said my words from the floor. It was ironic that when one of the pastors who wouldn't let me in the pulpit area found himself within hours of death, I was the chaplain who was called to his bedside. I think the shock of my face helped push him into heaven!

My grandmother Lucille is my only living grandparent. She has carried on my Granddaddy's legacy. She continues to fuss and remains close to all of us. My father and aunts take very good care of her. She checks on all of us. She keeps track of all the grands, great and now great, great grandchildren. She isn't much older than my Dad. She is younger than my mother. I don't know how I will feel if I outlive her. She represents the times in my life that were nurturing and kind. My paternal great grandfather and grandparents represent the fondest memories from my childhood.

Exposure to adult things in early childhood along with domestic violence in our home, significantly lowered my chances of having a productive life. This combination leaves one powerless and naked. It is like your body being turned inside out. You are vulnerable and hopeless. Not only do you not have inner strength and value but others tend to look upon you with pity and sometimes even disdain. I was mocked and ridiculed by the other kids for the way my parents interacted with one another. Their parents openly discussed what was going on in our home. Our home was not well kept. I should not have been subject to many things that took place in our home. The shame penetrated quite deep. The limits were crossed without my permission. I had to learn that I had value and power to set limits! This was a slow, painful process. I had to learn coping skills and discover what dignity and integrity are. My mother could not protect herself. She has never protected me. I grew to hate her. She was weak. I never hated my father, I was afraid of him. When I was around 16, he and I got into a physical fight. My mother had left my younger sister home alone. He thought it was my responsibility to care for her. I reminded him that he was her father, not I. After round one, I wasn't afraid of him or anyone else. My father taught me that no one would put his hands on me twice.

My sister and I were switched between two elementary schools when my mother would leave Daddy. I would often cry uncontrollably at school. My 5th grade teacher took time one afternoon to inform me that I could be *whatever I wanted to be in spite of my parents.* Her words have always stayed with me. My elementary school principal would let me sit in her office when I could not stop crying. I did not want to go home. I hated home. It really wasn't a home at all. I saw how the other girls lived. I could only imagine that kind of life. It seemed so far out of my reach.

I used to have this recurring dream. My father would cut up my mom. Then he would wash her in the sink with greens. She would be lost because no one would know she was in the greens. The beatings, the screaming, the blood. I would pretend God was with me. I pretended God was with me a lot. I am glad I had a good imagination. Then I could go back to sleep.

I finally met God in September 1979. I joined a Baptist church in June 1979 to keep my best friend from bugging me about coming to church. The pastor was saying something about Jesus not being able to find anyone that would go with him or work or something. Everyone had an excuse. I felt a bit bad myself, since I was headed for the tennis court. In fact, I was already running behind schedule. Before I knew it, I was walking down the aisle with my three young children. We joined church that day, however, Jesus continued to be a mystery to me. I figured he needed some help since no one else was helping him (Luke 9:60-62). Besides, how could I resist when this old gray haired man (the pastor) jumped up and down in excitement! He believed what he was saying and that was good enough for me. After many unanswered questions, I bought myself a Bible. Actually, I bought several

Bibles. I was quite the fashion plate in those days. I wanted a Bible to match my outfits. I did well with the outer appearance. The inside required a complete overhaul!

Knowing that I serve a risen Savior has been more real than the circumstances I was born into. I never doubted whether or not Christ died for me. I was so happy to know that God – someone, anyone – loved me! My youngest son, a sweet and mischievous child, talks happily about his childhood. I once read a paper he had written for one of his classes. He reports that although his father died when he was 9 years old, he has never known rejection. He continues to struggle with loneliness, but knows he was and is loved. My first husband and I planned to have him. I have never known that kind of love from a parent. We wanted a Christmas baby. He was born December 18. Just recently I insisted that my mother refrain from telling me that she did not want children. She did not have to tell me that. I lived it. Ephesians, Chapter One tells me that I am valued. My parents may not have known that children need to be nurtured. What matters is that I finally learned who I am meant to be.

My conversion experience was September 1979. I wanted to serve God. My theology was elementary but I knew Jesus really did die for me. Since death could not hold him in the grave, I took for granted that he could handle most anything. After learning the facts, it was easy for me to give my life to him. It was the least I could do. He gave his life for me. It sounded like a fair exchange. The Bible is not simply an ancient book or a myth collecting dust.

It is more real to me than the reality of my childhood. Salvation made good practical sense. I like being saved. My salvation saved me from myself.

I was attending a meeting shortly after I received Christ as my Savior. I was told that I would have more joy than the pain that I had carried all of my life. It proved to be true. This joy could only be given from God. God is real. I have never lost the joy of the Lord. His joy continues to be my strength regardless of what I am facing.

My life and my call to ministry are intertwined. I have the ordinations, formal education and professional credentials that validate my career in ministry. My calling is to be Christian. Regardless of my gifts or office in God's church and world, I must be Christian. Christianity is the means to help God unfold my life as he meant it to be. I am in partnership with God through Christ Jesus. It is from this relationship that I live my life.

Life is pretty good. The fifty years have been full of ups and downs. I just finished talking with my mom. She asked, "Have you heard from your Dad?" Just yesterday, I was talking with my dad, "Have you checked on your mom?" I suppose change isn't so bad. Yes, fifty is a good year.

The Awakening

It was too hard. There wasn't anything left. I had no energy, no willpower. I wanted it to be over. This morning was like all the others. I woke up. I wasn't with the Lord. If I could get to him, I would be healed. The pain would not leave me alone. I cried and longed for relief. Then I remembered the man at church who killed himself. Could this be the way he felt? I remembered it like it was yesterday. I always felt that we clergy staff weren't much help to his widow or daughters. How could he kill himself? He was tall, dark and quite dashing. An Ivy League Graduate. He had a good repertoire of credentials and achievements. He must have wanted out too. But why? Why did I want out? At that moment I knew I had to call his widow. It was in August. I had little energy. My husband brought me the telephone, looked up her number and dialed it for me. "Rev. Versey, where have you been?" she asked. I told her that I understood why he wanted to die. I felt the same way. I wasn't even sure why. Maybe he didn't know either. Why was I still alive? In the midst of my depression I had a paradigm shift. I had to live. I had to help others suffering from depression. The books were right. Something was terribly wrong inside of my brain. Stress had caught up with me. I didn't think things were that bad. I had everything to live for. If only my husband would get help for his mood swings. No two days had been the same since we married. It seemed he meant well, but it didn't feel good. I had no idea the biggest disappointment was many years down the road.

I began therapy in June of the same year. The headaches were pretty bad by then. I couldn't sleep or focus. Ministry inside the walls of a prison is special. Isaiah's words became alive (Isaiah 61)! Job fulfillment kept me going. It was inside those prison walls that God proved himself real and faithful among the men that had been condemned and many even forgotten. Prison ministry is not for the faint or unforgiving. The environment is ripe for stealing souls and encouraging hopelessness. It was there that I learned to love the *unloveable*. I learned how to forgive and taught others the same. I also learned that I too have flaws, faults and shortcomings. God does not stop loving us even when we end up behind bars. There is nothing so hideous that God cannot pardon. Sentences aren't dismissed but freedom flourishes from within! I was tremendously blessed by my work in prison ministry. My problems with a few staff were increasing. Soon my stomach churned, the aches and pains kept coming regardless of the Tylenol. I had to take some time off work. I missed going to the prison. God's spirit was moving in that place. I really learned that where there is sin, even more grace abounds. I also learned that we have stereotyped prisoners and staff. Whenever I hear prison staff or spokespersons say something negative about prison affairs, I am thankful that I had the opportunity to understand and see many things about the human condition.

I wasn't able to go back to work. I thought

a few weeks off would be sufficient. After awhile, I realized that the damage between prison staff and me could not be fixed. I was so mad at them! I really missed prison ministry. I missed the staff and the prisoners. I eventually let go and began to concentrate on getting well. My husband was endearing while I was sick. The only problem was that he would be close to me one minute, then cold as ice the next. How could he know how his mood swings affected me and not care? He had gotten medication to control his bipolar disorder but the side effects were too uncomfortable for him. When I found his almost full medication bottle two months later, I thought "his discomfort was nothing compared to the mood swings!" It was an uphill climb but I was willing to make adjustments since he obviously had no self control. I hadn't learned the true meaning of cruelty, but it was coming.

I was really excited when we married. It was the happiest day of my life. Everything was perfect. He was very romantic. I was doing a unit of Clinical Pastoral Education in another city. He drove up for dinner. My pager kept going off. He waited patiently. He asked me to marry him that night. He told me that God had spoken to him and I was his wfie. He wanted to spend the rest of his life with me. I had some concerns, but he had all the right answers. Yes, it would be a wonderful union! He was a real family man. He adored his children and parents. He spoke about them continually. His children's pictures were on his desk. My children were still in high school, college or dental school – all was supposed to be well. It was the complete opposite. In reality, he hadn't seen or spoken with either of his parents for many years. His relationship with his children was problematic at best. Their pictures were not current. It was obvious that he had few possessions. How could he have no financial assets or credit with such a generous salary? He gave me reasonable explanations for all of my concerns. I believed him. We decided that I would handle the finances since I obviously was a better money manger. I was able to overcome many hurdles from my childhood. Life was good. However, this was different. There was something wrong. Even so, the kindness he showed towards me during my breakdown helped me mend. Without him, I don't think I would have lived. I am sure that his bittersweet protection kept me alive. Protective one minute, mean as hell to me the next.

The voices told me that I wasn't worth much. I had failed at my calling. God couldn't use me anymore. Coupled with that dilemma, my isolation from work caused me to notice more about my husband than I could comprehend at the time. My husband always spoke highly of me but was growing colder and more distant. My marriage was not what it seemed to be. I knew he was bipolar but why was he absent for long periods of time with no explanation? Everything he did pointed towards another woman. We discussed his fidelity. He assured me that he was faithful. I believed him.

December of the same year gave me some relief. I decided that I had hurt long enough. I called my psychiatrist to let him know that I was tired of hurting. I was going to get a gun and kill all of the people from the prison that hurt me. I wanted my job back and I intended to have it. The list was pretty lengthy by then. As I reflect back, my husband wasn't on the list. I checked myself into the psychiatric ward. It sounds noble, but my psychiatrist urged me to go since I would be safe there. I felt like I was in the ocean treading water. My nose was just a bit above the water. I was gasping for breath. Two people or not, I needed my husband. I was all alone.

The hospital staff were a bit bewildered. They knew I was the on-call chaplain. I guess there aren't many chaplains who become psychiatric patients at the same hospital where they work. The weeks before, I couldn't manage the anger. I threw everything in sight. I would buy groceries. Instead of putting them away, I would throw them into the wall. I wanted the eggs to hurt so I smashed them into the wall. I wanted the milk to spill its guts. I wanted to rekill the meat. I stabbed it until I thought it was good and dead. During that period of time I would not let my granddaughter come around me. I was afraid that I might hurt her. A few times I pulled out all of the knives. I was going to cut my husband up piece by piece. I bet he wouldn't be moody then! Then I finally realized why he had mood swings! I was very close to my children, I thought he was having difficulty being away from his children. I felt really bad for wanting to cut him up. After all he couldn't help himself. He continued to show tenderness then without notice, he became the other person.

I walked to the hospital since it was only two blocks from my house. It was also safer than driving. For weeks I had urges to smash myself into oncoming traffic, especially the big trucks. The urges were getting stronger. Several times I had to stop and call my husband for help or get to a safe place. My first unit of Clinical Pastoral Education paid off. I used to ask God, "What's wrong with these people. I didn't understand why anyone would want to kill him or herself. Why can't they snap out of it?" God must have laughed. He knew I was headed for some first hand answers! I could not understand this clinical depression thing. I am thankful that I read everything I could get my hands on about the illness. I would listen for hours to the patients who told me their stories of worthlessness and pain. Their story had now become my own.

My roommate was a young woman who had tried to dispose of herself. I could relate to that. Except I wanted to dispose of some others along with me. I was not a very good mental patient. I questioned what my meds were before I would take them. The mean old nurse wouldn't give me the sheet that told the side effects of the drug that had been prescribed for me. She simply told me to take my meds. I learned fast that when you lose your mind, some people do not think you have any sense. The pill my doctor prescribed for me knocked me out for a few hours but waking up was a trip. I felt like a spider crawling sideways up the wall. It was awful. I *crawled* to the nursing station and asked how long the drug would stay in my system. No one thought it necessary to answer my question. Did I look that crazy? I then insisted that they page the doctor. Yeah, right. I phoned him later that morning. From that time forward I was aware of the side effects of my meds. I did not like mind altering drugs. What little sanity I had left was worth keeping!

I learned much from my roommate. She told me why she wanted to end her life. Her boyfriend was going to leave her. The thought of being left alone was too overwhelming. "Something inside of me shrivels up and dies when there is not a man in my life." "He must have been very good to you." "No, he was awful. He beat the crap out of me all of the time." So much for goodness. The awakening had begun. I too had shriveled up and died inside. I had no career. Then I realized that although my husband did not hit me, I felt the blows nonetheless. Wow. Somehow I couldn't see myself as she was. She was weak and pitiful. Her pajamas did not even match. I was well dressed – pajamas with a matching robe, house slippers and arrogance. She had no insurance. I was educated, well trained, and fully insured. I had working relationships with hospital staff. I wasn't like her. Or was I?

Suddenly my matching pajamas and robe could not mask my pain and humiliation. I was just like her. I could absolutely relate to her plight. My husband paid the bills but he certainly did not love me. Did he? Could he ignore how his moods affected us and still love me? Couldn't he see how my family and friends were distancing themselves from me? What in the world happened to me? At one time I had a good life. I had many accomplishments and triumphs. Life had always been a challenge for me but it was always tolerable. I did not want to be empty but I did not know how to fill the void. I had been neglected as a child but no one treated me the way my husband was treating me. My dreams, my career, my fairy tale wedding, the husband that I adored, it was all a lie. I kept it close to my aching heart. What was I to do? My husband was bipolar. Why he would not seek help was beyond me. I would have to live with his disorder.

Some of my best moments were while I was upon my bed of affliction. The several days I spent in the mental health unit were nice. I rather enjoyed the arts and craft time. Music therapy and making collages were nice too. Group time was great! Having people who actually spoke to me every day was wonderful! No one hurt me there. I had almost two really nice weeks. No one could come near me without my permission. No prison staff, no one. I did not want to go home. My husband would come and visit me. I remember once he cried while we were visiting. I remember wondering why he was crying. He was sometimes mean as hell to me. I joked with my roommate. We needed to take her boyfriend and my husband and sedate them permanently. Why and how could a person put you through hell and feel compassion for you at the same time?

The first two years of my illness I had little energy. It was also difficult to focus. Those were lonely years. My husband and I never shared a bedroom. He preferred to stay in the basement. I couldn't blame him. I had tastefully decorated it for him. However, I had also tastefully decorated our bedroom. I carefully selected furniture that he would be comfortable in since he was a bit tall. I even had all of his family pictures enlarged and framed. He had his very own picture gallery. I was tired of seeing them in the worn brown envelope. They were undressed, they needed frames! He had his very own everything; I made certain he was very comfortable. It wasn't a chore at all. I liked being a homemaker. I liked being his wife. I loved him. I was glad to be in our very own home. He had moved into my house when we married. He did not like the neighborhood, the furniture or anything else in our old house. He would stay up all night. He just did not like it there. I eagerly found a house that he could afford. This way he would feel better. That was the answer. Since I had more assets than he, it was uncomfortable for him to live in my house. During that time, I also did some things with my sister's children. I wasn't able to stay home with my own children when they were school aged. I rather liked having them around. They weren't around long. My husband grew intolerant of them. They were a bit spoiled. I could see my husband's point. I also helped my sister decorate her new home. Whatever I could do, I did it. I didn't have much energy but I used what I had. My husband did not like my white living room furniture so I tastefully decorated my sister's house with it. As I reflect on that time, I laugh. He always complained about my taste in decorating with colors. He is color blind! None of the furniture in his apartment matched. Most of it was given to him. He was quite picky to have so little. I was really glad to move. Perhaps his moods would improve and he would stay home more. Where did he disappear for so long? Besides, I do like shopping. I had to buy new things for our new house!

By the time we moved into our new house, I

knew he was not able to handle money. He always gave me money for the household account. He went through money like water, (The manic side of his mood disorder). He would produce no goods or services. We had some discussions about his inability to manage money. He said he was sending money to his children on top of the child support he was paying. It was understandable. I also had children, they are expensive.

Aside from his job he had little interest in a social life. He had those few close friends. I had never seen a man who spent so much time with other men. They never traveled or had projects, they just hung out in the basement. My husband wasn't able to concentrate on outside activities long, they couldn't hold his interest. He was an excellent basketball player. Several times he started the season assisting a friend of ours but wouldn't follow through the season. There would always be a problem with parents, staff or children. It saddened me, he would have made a tremendous coach for youth. After we were married, I learned that he frequently missed work. We had a short conversation about his absenteeism. I am not a workaholic but my parents instilled a good work ethic in me. For a season he really tried to go to work faithfully. Sometimes he just couldn't get up and go to work. His mood disorder really got the best of him. His moods affected me the worst. It was my burden to bear, "For better or for worse." Worse eventually destroyed better. I gave up trying to get him to take medication. It was futile. I talked, I begged, I cried and began to distance myself from him when I could not bear his mood. Even so, he remained protective during those years of my recuperation. He accompanied me to the doctor and saw to it that I kept myself up. If he could just get a handle on those mood swings, we would have some good days. We would be able to plan for our future. We could have a social life. Whatever plans we had, his mood would preclude him from following through. In front of others he was nice to me. It changed as soon as we left their sight.

The dark nights of the soul were long. I did not sleep regularly for over a year. I was beyond tired but couldn't sleep. My nerves and bones ached. Since my husband had no interest in me personally, I found things to do. It was during these three years of illness that I learned how to decorate cakes, arrange floral pieces and play the piano. I didn't like being around people much, but I liked to see the beauty of a finished product. Between cake decorating, floral arrangements and piano, the dark nights weren't so dark. I could play the hymns of the church all through the night. My husband complained about almost everything, but he never complained about me trying to play the piano. I remember how the music would lift me above the pain. And the Psalms – the comfort of the 139th and the assurance of the 27[th.] The psalmist cried out to the Lord and so did I. The Lord heard us both. I learned to appreciate the simple things of God. Had I remained ill, I would be an excellent pianist now! I wasn't able to attend church services. I was still afraid of people and the noise really bothered me. My goal became to attend the early morning service. I missed receiving Holy Communion and kneeling at the altar to pray. I would get there in just enough time to walk the aisle and kneel at the chancel rail. There was no magic in the wood but I knew that my God would meet me there. It reminded me of the Ark of the Covenant. Above the testimony was the atonement cover. On top were the cherubim. There, God would meet his people as they traveled towards the promised land. Above my head was the cross. My name was written on that cross. Jesus knew what I was going through. He was pierced for my transgressions and bruised for my iniquities. The chastisement of my peace was upon him and by his stripes I would be healed. Time and the Lord were on my side. I would be well again. Church was safe. It was the only place that my husband could not hurt me. I had thought him to be a Christian when we married. He was from the Baptist tradition but at his insistence he joined me in the Methodist tradition. He did not attend church for many years. He had no interest in the life of our church. His absence from church initially was very disappointing and embarrassing. Why could he spend so much time with his friends and not with his wife? After a while I was grateful for the peace away from him.

There were some new insights and adventures. I missed ministry. I often kept in touch with prison staff to see how certain men were doing inside the walls. My heart went out the men who were my children's ages. I still prayed for the prisoners and the staff. There was a great void after I left the prison. Where did I belong?

I began to concentrate solely on getting well enough to go back to work. With my husband's help and the advice of my therapist, I began to plot out the little triumphs that would help me gain some confidence, strength and courage. Slowly I began to feel better about myself. I really missed receiving gifts. My husband rarely gave me presents. He gave me a red rose to celebrate our first week anniversary. I don't remember him giving me any other gift. In the first year or so of our marriage he did give me beautiful cards. I missed being treated like a woman. I longed to be held. I begged him to sleep with me. I was so lonely. I took it quite personally when the cable bill would come. He watched X-rated movies while in the basement. Why would he watch X-rated movies when he had a wife? Why was he sleeping in the basement instead of with me? First, he said he missed his waterbed. I purchased a waterbed. The mattress was too soft. The new firm mattress became too hard for his back. Then he blamed my lack of housekeeping for his absence. Finally, he kicked me out of the bedroom altogether. All of this was too painful and too hard. My husband did not find me desirable. I prayed and asked God to fill the void with his love for me. Soon the emptiness left. I began to find little pleasures for myself. I always showered before my breakdown. During my illness, I didn't have much energy to stand or much desire to take a shower for that matter. My husband encouraged me to take a bath instead of trying to stand in the shower. To this day, I still take a bubble bath every day. I take time for me. I began to buy cut flowers and arrange them perfectly for my kitchen table. For years there were always fresh flowers on my table. My husband once picked some up when I wasn't feeling well enough to drive. I appreciated his kindness. I have a dear friend (she remains close to me this day) who helped me gain an appreciation of what it means to be a woman. My husband's rejection wounded me deeply.

I dreaded holidays and those special days when couples and families were supposed to be together. My husband would disappear for most of the day. We spent a part of a Thanksgiving one year with dear friends and as a family we spent two wonderful holidays together, Thanksgiving and Christmas in the year he had been injured in a car accident. He was confined to the bed – on his back. Those were the best seven months we had. My family also appreciated this time. A wonderful man was inside of the simmering volcano. There was not one mood swing in seven months. It didn't last, but those months were really nice.

I can gauge my progress towards getting well by the Annual Conferences I was required to attend for my denomination. I had to answer the roll call for Itinerant Elders. The first August I could not walk the long aisle to be seated in the section for clergy. I had little energy. I could not sit up. I ached badly. I leaned on my husband and answered the roll call from my seat. After I answered roll call, my husband drove me home. The second August was a better year. I could not drive. I rode with one of the members of our church. She took very good care of me. I could not keep up with a schedule, however, I was able to attend some of the sessions. The third August was a good one. I was driving my car again but was still too nervous for expressway driving. I rode with our pastor. I actually stayed the entire business session of the Conference! My husband came to join me on the Friday of the second and third Conferences. We never stayed until the Conference closed. The second year he was in such a bad mood that he refused to be cordial to those who tried to extend a welcome to him. He was angry and rude to my colleagues. I was so hurt. Why would he embarrass me in front of my colleagues when I was so kind to his friends? My husband and I left together early. For my own sake, I needed to get him away from my colleagues. The third year when I rode to Conference with our pastor, my husband joined me at the end of the week. We enjoyed a lovely dinner with my daughter and her friend. It was my birthday. Before we got back to our hotel from dinner, his mood had swung. He was no longer speaking to me. He was angry. He seldom slept at night. That night was no exception. He woke me up around 5 AM. He demanded that I take him to the bus station. He actually caught a bus back home, less than one hour away. He got directions from someone and off we went at 5 AM. I hadn't driven in a big city since my breakdown. I was shaking when I returned to my hotel room. It was also the first time since my illness that I had to face expressway driving. I cried all the way home. I had to stop three times to compose myself. But I made it home. I knew then I could push a little further towards recovery.

We have never had an overnight trip that did not end with a violent mood swing. As soon as we would get home, he would disappear. He would either cut the trip short or his behavior was so anti-social that I tried really hard to get him back home. He hadn't seen either of his parents in many years. Our first year of marriage, we went to visit his father and step-mother. They are a wonderful couple! After a few days, he stopped speaking to me except in the presence of his parents or others. By the time we left he was angry and agitated. He was eager to get back home. We traveled across the country four years later to visit with his children and mother. It was my gift to him. This would be the first time seeing his mother in many, many years. It was nice meeting his mother. His youngest daughter was graduating. We traveled by Amtrak. It began as a wonderful trip. The first two nights of traveling were good. Our first night in the hotel room was good. After graduation, we went over to his former wife's home. Her family welcomed me. I spent most of my time with his son. I bought tickets for us to visit the Aquarium in their city. We had several other field trips planned. My husband and his former wife's friends were there too. Everyone was laughing and listening to music. It was a nice evening, the house was full of life. It seemed all was well. Something happened. That night he refused to sleep in the hotel room. He actually slept in the car until we left a few days later. He wanted to be by himself. I promised myself that it would be our last trip together. He refused to drive me to pick up his son for our field trips. When I decided to drive myself, he forbade me from picking up his son. He also called his son and ordered him not to see me. He wouldn't even go back to visit his children before we left their city. He needed help and I was not willing to be subjected to his behavior any longer. When it was time for us to leave, he would not go with me to return the rental car. He wanted to be dropped off at the train station early in the morning. Our train left early evening. After returning the rental car, I walked over three miles with my luggage back to the train station since he would not watch my luggage along with his. It never occurred to me to get a cab. We were on the other side of the country. I phoned my dear friend every chance I could. I needed someone to talk me back home. The trip home on the Amtrak was embarrassing. We dined with other travelers. My husband would not engage in conversation with anyone – even when spoken to. I was alone, scared and tired of being mistreated. It was also during this time that I began to move money so he did not have easy access to it. It was simply practical. There was no discussion, it was futile. We would never have anything if I allowed him to continue his spending with no accountability.

By the end of the third year of my illness, I was able to visit some patients at the hospital. I had been on call at two local hospitals before I fell apart. I arranged to make visits a few hours a week. I pushed a little further. Things at home were beginning to get on my nerves in a healthy sort of way. I always liked homemaking. I enjoyed cooking and doting over my husband. I laid his suits and accessories out each day for work. I even polished his shoes! Even so, there was little that I did that met his approval but I continued to try. One morning he kicked me out of his bedroom even though he slept in the basement. I refused to do anything for a few days. Before long,

I was back to doting over him. I was entrenched in co-dependency. Usually I cooked both his breakfast and dinner. He did not like leftovers. There were many times that he walked past his breakfast. I used to wonder why he couldn't simply tell me that he wasn't hungry. Silly me. By then he seldom talked to me at all. How could I expect him to be considerate of my breakfast and dinner detail? As I gained strength, I also became more intolerable of his behavior towards me. It was an uphill climb but I was on a steady mend.

I actually got pretty good at dodging the verbal bullets of steel. There was once a time it would take days to rise above his terse insults. His violent mood swings could occur at anytime. He would be calm one minute and threatening the next. He was like a tornado touching down, he did not care how his words or demeanor effected me. In response to my asking him to consider me, he would quickly snap, "I only care about me." There was one occasion his co-worker was visiting. I had prepared a wonderful meal for them. I loved cooking for him and his company. As his company was leaving I remembered dessert. My husband was already going down the basement stairs. At my beckoning, our guest returned for his dessert. Standing at the top of the steps, I asked my husband if he wanted a piece of cake. He cursed me and told me to close his damn door. Our guest heard him. He was shocked. He shared that my husband always spoke so highly of me at work. Our guest saw the other person. Still, it was difficult to believe that my husband was playing such a cruel game. That incident helped me distance myself from my husband a little further. I was getting stronger.

I hadn't been able to attend seminary prior to my ordinations. One morning a sweet voice awakened me, "Go to seminary." I talked it over with my husband. Bless his heart. He never stood in my way. He just made it extremely hard for me to stand! Soon after I began school, he went on a cleaning rampage. He threw out all of my arts and crafts material and some of my dried and silk flowers. He didn't like clutter. He always reminded me of my housekeeping inadequacies. He gathered up my hobby items and put them in a trash bag. He made sure I would not get them back. He hauled them away. No one had ever thrown out my possessions before. That really hurt. I felt so violated. How could he throw out my things when I had provided so much for him?

I took my hurt feelings and pushed a little further. Soon it became no big deal. His criticism had lost its potency. When the house was perfectly clean he didn't notice or it still wasn't clean enough. The food was either too hot or too cold. The vegetables were either too soft or too hard. Nothing pleased him. I needed more. It was apparent that my husband could not control his behavior. What the heck. It was my time!

Rebuilding

*O*ff to seminary I went. I enrolled in the Masters of Arts, Educational Ministry program. I was able to complete the program in three years since I had two units of Clinical Pastoral Education. My CPE satisfied my field experience requirements. At the urging of my husband I lived on campus most of the week. The first few weeks I would lay out his outfits for the week. (Whenever I needed to be away I laid out his clothing before I left home.) I came home one day and he was in the basement fast asleep. I called him from the top of the stairs. He was knocked out. The upstairs wasn't clean. He was the only one home. Why wasn't he at work? Why hadn't he worn any of the clothing I laid out for him?

I actually liked being away from home. I was around people who talked to me. We shared our experiences. We laughed. I felt alive again! I hadn't felt that good since I was in the mental institution. Seldom did I talk with my husband during those two years. I would call him at work but often he was not there. The embarrassment of not knowing where he was stopped my calling him at work. He wasn't reachable at home either. Throughout our marriage, the phone could ring forever right next to him but he wouldn't answer it. I was dining one afternoon while away at school. A mutual friend teased me that I would flunk out of school if my husband did not stay home and let me get some homework done. The joke was on me. He never visited me while I was in school.

He phoned me once to tell me that he would no longer be giving me money for the household account. I expected it. I stopped giving him extra spending money. When I had extra money I would put it in his account. In error, I got a printout of his checking account. I panicked. It thought someone was taking money out of my checking account continuously. When I questioned the teller, I realized it was his account. He had more spending money than I had for the household budget, yet he often borrowed from the household account. I moved money to another bank where he would no longer have easy access to it. When he withdrew money from my account, I expected him to replace it. I was no longer cooking, cleaning and making life comfortable for him. I did what I could between terms but I had clearly become my own priority.

When I graduated, some of the ladies at church gave me a luncheon at my apartment. Some of the guests asked him for directions to my apartment. He had no idea where I lived.

Graduation was great. The two years sped by. It was my turn for the open house. Two of my children, grandchildren, daughter-in-law and several friends came to help me celebrate. I enjoyed my seminary experience. The thought of living in the same house with my husband again was not appealing. I had become accustomed to people who cared about one another and me. My husband's urging me to stay on campus gave him considerable freedom. His freedom proved to be a good thing. He was really sweet at my graduation. As usual, he was the highlight of the luncheon. He told me he was very proud of me. As moody as he was, he was also to be commended. He helped me achieve my goal. I moved home later that evening. By morning he was different (again). Desperate, I knelt at my bedside three days later, "Lord, please show me why my husband treats me like this and I ask that you break him from it." I prayed on Thursday. I found his drugs and paraphernalia days later. He left them in a dessert dish in one of the coffee table drawers in the basement. Sometimes we don't get the answers or the outcomes that we expect from God. I was decorating a cake and needed a toothpick to color some icing. While looking for the toothpick, I stumbled upon what I thought was his candy stash. When I reached back in the drawers I thought, "Ooo I found the good candy." He always had sweets. I was excited to find the good stuff! Instead, what I found took my breath away. It was like someone had hit me really hard in the pit of my stomach. It made me sick. I threw up. I finally had the answer. I knew the truth. It was a relief. I wasn't a terrible housekeeper. I really could iron his shirts right. All of those things that I could never do right were right. He had mistreated me, my children, my family, my friends for his drug high. The many times I begged him to answer me, it was as though I wasn't there. He ignored me; it was as though he was in another world. The missing money; his daughter was telling the truth when she insisted her father was not sending her money regularly. Were his friends borrowing that much money? What happened to the $1,000.00 I put in his account? Why was it withdrawn in less than two days with nothing to show for it? He wasn't bipolar. My husband was strung out. I knew it. I learned this term from the prisoners. The drug was like a trail. It was leading him. It had total control of his life.

Even though I had the answers, it seemed impossible. What about his position at work, his anti-drug stance? He told me repeatedly that he opposed drugs. He knew I held drugs in disdain. We had conversations about drugs when we married. Drugs destroyed people's lives. They hurt families. He couldn't be using drugs. It must be his friends. All the times his friends came over, it was his friends that were getting high, not him. How could they get high in our home? I cooked dinner for them. I set the downstairs table for them to eat. I was good to them too. He was letting his friends get high in our home. I couldn't quite understand why he would let such a thing happen but I would get to the bottom of the whole thing. I finally had some answers. I had the evidence, but I didn't know what all of it was. I knew the razor blade and straw was for cocaine. I couldn't quite understand what the toilet paper roll was with the hole. I could see that something had been burned on top of the foil. The aluminum-foiled packet was closed. I was afraid to open it.

As a child, I had been afraid of my father. I was scared when I found myself clear across the country with an angry, strange acting husband. This was the first time I became afraid of him. I had been introduced to a new world. My husband clearly was not on my side. He had more than proven that his loyalty was not with me.

I discovered that night that there is a bit of Sherlock Holmes in me. I took pictures of what I found. I picked each article up with the tips of my fingers. I was shaking. I had to talk to myself to calm down. After I took the pictures, I left everything on the dessert dish as I had found it. I neatly placed it on the coffee table. I phoned my attorney. It was almost midnight. I also phoned the police department and spoke with an officer. They both assured me that the odds were against me. He would probably get rid of me before he would stop getting high. History wasn't in my favor. Both told me that the objects I found were used for cocaine and probably crack. No way, it could not be crack. I really thought my husband would tell me everything. I had the evidence. Surely, he was a man of his word. I had believed him all those years. I was a good wife to him. He had so little when we married, he was comfortable now. Why would he deliberately do this to me? I took the film and the important papers that would prove the house was legally mine too and gave them to someone whom I could trust. The police officer thought my husband would either hurt me physically or try to run me away from the house. This is what drug addicts do when they are threatened. This was so far out of my realm of thinking. The officer took my name and address. I had the name and the cell phone numbers of two policemen just in case.

I made a few phone calls looking for my husband. I was ready for some answers. No one had seen him. When he arrived home, I met him at the door. I confronted him about my discovery. He walked over to the kitchen sink. He turned on the water. He couldn't look at me. He took the dishtowel and began to wash a clean sink. He became defensive and vulgar. He refused to answer me. "Why are there drugs in our home?" "What is that toilet paper thing?" He told me to mind my own business. "This is my house too", I reminded him. Actually, my husband never regarded our house as my home. I had abided by his rules for years to keep peace. It was better to give in than deal with his temper and moods. He brushed past me. He had never done that before. Each time he passed by me until his accident, he made certain that he brushed me out of the way. When I had to walk past him, I stayed at a distance until he was well past me. I was scared. They were right. The battle had intensified.

The next morning I called my father-in-law for advice. He and I were more like father and daughter. He was heartbroken. History was repeating itself. He urged me to call my husband's job and tell them what I had found. I couldn't do it. Perhaps there was a reasonable explanation for what I found? Denial had been become my way of life. Since my husband would not answer my questions, I called the substance abuse clinic. I described what I found. The other thing was a homemade crack pipe. I could not believe it. Denial is when all of the evidence is there, but you just won't believe it. I didn't believe that my husband, the anti-drug person, was smoking crack-cocaine too. The truth is that I had been in denial since a few days after our wedding. The signs were all there. The problem was that I stereotyped what a drug addict looked like. Drug addicts weren't well dressed. In reality, before we married, my husband had one suit that his sister had purchased for him. I very carefully made certain that he was a well-dressed man. From head to foot, he matched perfectly. He had to. I required that he be well-dressed both causally and professionally. No one left my house looking unkempt. It was a rule. Ask my kids. I had been co-dependent from day one. I meticulously purchased all of his clothing. I also insisted that he reconcile with his parents and other relatives. I planned all the trips for him to spend time with them! I managed his money and mine! The money for the down payment for our house was from funds I had prior to marrying my husband. I enabled my husband to walk all over me while he nursed his lover. Still, I refused to believe that he was a crack addict. Perhaps cocaine but not crack! My mind kept flashing back to the stories I heard from the prisoners, "You can't dress up a crack head, you must confront the addiction." My God, I had dressed up crack. I prepared meals for crack. Crack-cocaine lived an enjoyable life at my expense. All of this was overwhelming for me.

Determined to get a more acceptable answer, I had the pictures developed and took copies to the substance abuse clinic. It was confirmed again. I didn't know whether to cry or run. All those years, he abused me to get high? What about his position? What about all those talks we had? I phoned him at work. I told him that I knew what the toilet paper thing was and I knew what he was doing with it. He hung up on me. When he came home that afternoon, he had removed his wedding ring. The stakes had been raised to another level.

Each time I tried to talk with him, he would ignore or curse me. He assured me that he would put me out of his house. Between the time I found his drugs and his accident, he never spoke one civil word to me. His whole demeanor changed. He didn't even try to control his disdain for me. It was as though he hated me. I wasn't the one hurting him. I loved him. I was scared of him. One evening I heard a car pull up in our driveway. I looked out the window to see who it was. I actually thought it was my daughter. I went to the door to meet her. My husband had put her out of our home earlier in the year. I was concerned that he would insult her. She hadn't been over since he took her key to our house and made her move her things out. She lived in another city. She and I didn't realize that her house key infringed upon his freedom. With me away in school, he didn't have to stay so long in the downstairs bathroom. I always wondered why he stayed so long in that bathroom. It wasn't my daughter at the door. It was the friend my husband visited regularly. It was the friend who lived one hour away – the same city where I was in seminary. He past by my apartment to get to his house. Early in our marriage, my husband confided to me that he used drugs. Since he knew I didn't like drugs he wouldn't let him visit or call our home. My husband was good. This friend never visited our home the entire time we were married. He wasn't going to start now. In fact, I called all of my husband's friends and let them know there would be no more getting high in our house. Some of them told him about our conversation. My husband told me if I did not stop running my mouth, he would close it for me. It was obvious that I had developed some courage along the way. I would not be mistreated for crack. I confronted his friend at the door. "Do you have drugs? You aren't going to bring drugs in our home." By then my husband was coming up from the basement. He pushed me inside the kitchen and closed the door. I was bewildered. Why was he defending his friend? I was his wife. I could hear them in the basement talking about me. I started pleading the blood of Jesus on my husband's life. The man couldn't stay. I heard him say, "Man I can't stay here. It's too hot for me to stay here." He left and my husband threatened me. He gently pressed his finger to my chest and forgot my name. "Bitch, I will put you out of here tomorrow." "This is my house."

Forgiveness

That was hard. The man I adored called me a bitch. He preferred his friend and his crack to me. It was the ultimate insult and rejection. Another layer of unspeakable pain to digest. This one was too hard for me. I walked over to my glider. I sat and rocked a few minutes. I wouldn't let the tears come this time. I forgave my husband for calling me a bitch. I forgave him for mistreating me. I had to forgive him. Crack and cocaine had destroyed our marriage, but I had something to say about what it continued to do to me. It wasn't going to destroy me. I forgave him for my own survival. Forgiveness freed me to continue living without adding another layer of unspeakable pain to my already wearied soul.

A few weeks later, I was headed for our church's General Conference. It was only five hours away that year. My husband assured me that all of my possessions would be gone when I returned home. I begged and pleaded with him not to carry out his threats. I took pictures of my possessions and our home. I walked around the house pleading the blood of Jesus on it and my possessions. I knelt down and prayed that God would protect me, my husband and the house while I was absent. While I was away, I had a dream. In the dream, my youngest son received a telephone call. One of his friends wanted him to hang out with him. He left and had got in a car accident. He died. When I awakened from the dream, I immediately rebuked death and prayed the will of God for his young life. I also phoned him. I told him not to leave home late at night and the reason why. He promised he would not leave home to party and would also be careful in his travels. The day I arrived home, my aunt and cousin came over my our house. My husband insulted my aunt and cousins. They spoke to him. He ignored them. They tried to engage in conversation with him, he refused to acknowledge their presence. I wanted to die. As usual, I justified his behavior. He left home late that evening. I didn't know he was gone. He left sometime after 10 PM since I went to bed about that time. He was still in the basement when I retired for the evening. I woke up around 4 AM startled by a bang. Someone hit a utility pole, the whole neighborhood was pitch black. The electricity was out. I looked out of the kitchen window. His car was gone. This was the first time he stayed out all night. He would come home late, but he never stayed out all night. I cried out to God (again). It was too much. I needed his help. Drugs, being threatened, the name calling, and now I thought, "a real another woman." It was too much. I felt so alone (again). I was afraid of my own shadow by then. I was already barricading myself in my bedroom each night since my discovery. Each night I prayed myself to sleep asking for God's protection from my husband.

The telephone rang about 8:30 AM. It was the hospital. "Mrs. ?" "Yes." "Your husband wanted me to call you. He has been in a car accident. He will need surgery, his leg is broken." "What happened?" "He was in a car accident but we can't operate until his alcohol level comes down." I sat down on the hallway floor. I cried tears of relief. For the first time in years, I knew he wouldn't be able to hurt me for at least one day. He was in the same city where I attended school. No doubt he had been on his way to his friend's house. The nurse told me to take my time, it would take hours before he could go into surgery. I went to the hospital that afternoon. His injuries were extensive. He would need more surgeries. He would need care to recuperate. There were some doubts as to whether or not he would walk again. It seemed so strange to be referred to as his *wife*. The last words from him assured me that he would burn the house down with me in it. I don't think he remembered my name wasn't bitch – until he needed me to take care of him. It was a bitter pill but I eventually swallowed it.

I was afraid to stay home alone the first week he was hospitalized. I wasn't quite sure how far he was going to take his threats. My children were also scared for me. My daughter was scheduled to attend a conference for her profession. She arranged for me to accompany her. It was strange letting her protect me. I was relieved to be away. It was hard not to defend my actions. It looked like I abandoned my helpless husband in the time of his need. I was trying to survive. He was not helpless at all. He had just become more manageable. Whether an act of God or because he was drunk and driving, his injuries gave my family and me some much needed relief from his abuse and cruelty. I didn't know he drank heavily. It was obvious to me that I had no idea what actually went on down in the basement. I gathered his belongings from the hospital and prayed that God would help me begin the journey for his recuperation. He was in the hospital two months. He wanted to get well. He was the highlight of therapy. He was always the highlight in public. It was only in private that his true self emerged. His assigned social worker picked up that I was uneasy and kept my distance from him. She also knew he was a drug user and his drug of choice was cocaine. I never told hospital staff that he was a drug addict. She gave me some information about drug rehabilitation possibilities. The hospital chaplain also helped me decide if I would be able to take care of my husband after he left the hospital. After speaking with his surgeon I was reasonably secure. He would be bedridden for many months. If I kept my distance, it would be difficult for him to hurt me. I was pleasantly surprised. He needed me to take of him so he wasn't going to jeopardize his needs. He was manageable. I was so hoping that his accident would deter him for using drugs and alcohol.

The friends that I barred from our home visited him regularly in the hospital. There were several times they were in his room when I visited him. I would leave the hospital and go home. I tried staying with him overnight a few times. It was too hard. His oldest daughter phoned me one afternoon to see how I was doing. "I know how hard it is to live with my dad, how are you doing?" I cried. No one ever asked me how I was doing. All attention was focused on my husband. He was good. He was the victim. Did he forget how he had treated me? To my surprise, he actually thought I should have been more attentive while he was in the hospital. Does crack-cocaine give one amnesia? I couldn't be around him for weeks. I couldn't stomach his friends or his pretenses. I graciously answered everyone's questions like a good wife should. I didn't want to see him. I cared for him at a distance. I made sure he had enough clothes for the week. I tailored his pants to fit the apparatus on his leg. I bought him shirts he could easily maneuver since his arm and shoulder were also severely injured. I made the two hour round trip each week to wash his clothes and meet with his medical caregivers. I spoke with his therapists and nurses frequently. I was there for the important meetings about his care. I would buy him meals if he had a taste for something other than what the hospital offered. On one visit, my husband's childhood friend discerned my pain. He phoned me at home. I was defensive and guarded. He shared he was once a drug addict. My husband had jokingly told him early in our marriage that I wouldn't know a drug if it were in front of me. My husband knew me well. I asked the friend why he was calling me. He said I reminded him of the women he once abused for his addiction. Since he was sober he now understood the damage he did while using. He apologized for my husband's behavior. He said a prayer for me. I cried.

While my husband was in the hospital I suggested that he go to drug rehabilitation, assuring him I would stand by him. I really loved my husband. He became defensive, almost called me a bitch but caught himself. After all, he needed me to take care of him. I left his hospital room and did not return until the day of his discharge. I did not want him to come back home. While he was away, I could open widows and doors. I could watch any television program I wanted to watch. My family and friends still stayed away but I had the whole house without rule or regulation. On his trial visit home from the hospital, the therapist and I were walking around the house. The handicapped ramp had just been built for his wheelchair. I was wheeling him with us. When we past by the patio he asked why I hadn't planted flowers or cut the grass. He was good. He had not allowed me to plant flowers that year. He also forbade me from cutting the grass. It was his patio and his grass. It was then I realized I was a prisoner in my own home. He had been in the hospital almost two months and I was still obeying some of his rules to keep peace. He was good at pretending we were a couple in public. How I wish he could have loved me the way he loved his crack. I would be one happy and completely satisfied woman.

When he came home, he couldn't do much for himself. I bathed him, emptied his toilet, dressed his wounds, made certain he took his medication, drove him to his appointments, I picked up where I left off. I did it all over again. I wanted him to get well. My mother would prepare his meals and sit with him when I had to be gone more than a few hours. It was interesting seeing him manageable. He never apologized to me for the way he treated me. Even so, I nursed him back to enough health that when able, he arranged to be picked up by the ones who were no longer welcome in our home. He had volunteered one of them to cut the grass and then when the snow fell, to clean the driveway. I told him that I was not secure with them around me. Drugs would not come back into our home. Since my husband needed semi-skilled care, our Insurance Company compensated me for some of his care. I wasn't comfortable being paid to take care of him. I promised God that I would cherish him in sickness and in health. The company's representative was constantly reminding me to send in the forms to get paid. He faxed me the forms at work one afternoon. I saved every penny of that money. Little did I know that I would use it to hire an attorney to represent me when my husband filed for divorce.

I enjoyed being married to him minus the mood swings, abuse and cruelty. There wasn't much else left but I am thankful for the few good moments we shared. For seven months there was peace in our home. He was balanced. Not one mood swing until he left with his friends again. The more he recovered, the more controlling and demanding he became. I broke my thumb putting his wheelchair in the trunk of my car. When I picked him up from therapy after getting my thumb set, he complained about my being late. The signs were slowly emerging again. The substance abuse counselors were right. If he showed no remorse, he probably was headed for his drug of choice. The longer crack stays out of your system, the more you crave it. I was foolish enough to think that he wanted to get well for us. I asked him if the bad times were behind us. I believed him again.

My husband thrived on the attention he received. Visitors, flowers, prayers, he was a hero. He even began attending church. He seldom attended before his accident. I wanted to scream when I heard him tell how he was hit by a car trying to help others. He left out that he was the one who hit the other car and that he was drunk. When he was in the hospital, the police officer came to arrest him for drunk driving. Since he was in surgery, I made arrangements for him to be under house arrest. He would eventually appear in court for his drunk driving charge. I made arrangements to postpone his arraignment until his health was better. Several months later, before his sentencing, the judge asked if I wanted to address the court. I wanted to stand up and shout, "Don't believe him, he's lying and please make him stop hurting me!" Instead I politely said, "No Your Honor." He was good. He told the judge he was just having an *off night* and had too much to drink. Addiction had taught him how to lie, manipulate and destroy with ease. I was no better. I was a model example of how a co-dependently, abused wife should behave in the presence of her abuser and the public.

By the time his moods were in full swing, I had a new attitude. I wasn't afraid of him anymore. I was willing to love and cherish him but not the crack. Before his leg apparatus was removed, he began to enjoy his newfound freedom. Since I wouldn't let his barred friends near the house - not even in the driveway - he arranged to have friends I hadn't barred from the house pick him up, wheelchair and all! Nothing I did was good enough, but I wasn't the same person he walked over for his lover, crack. I loved him dearly, but he wasn't going to sacrifice me again. I stood my ground. No drug friends or drugs were coming in our house. And he would no longer mistreat me. I agonized over not doing anything else for him. I didn't realize it at the time but I was beginning to break free from our co-dependent relationship. I prayed for almost two months that God would give me enough strength to not let him continue mistreating me. By then I resented him. He hadn't changed, he needed me to take care of him. I tried to reason with him. I told him that he was hindering his own health. He couldn't get well mistreating me. His anger took up energy that needed to be positively channeled for him to get well. I was not his enemy. He snapped, "Then I just won't get well." He was still in his wheelchair. I was stunned. He reacquainted himself with his lover. This time he and his lover had to leave the house to meet. Drugs were not coming into my house. God answered my prayer. I actually went my first 24 hours without doing anything for him unless he asked. Since he was able to go out with his friends, he was able to do some things for himself. He was furious. He began punishing me right away. He didn't want me to do anything at all for him. He pushed me completely away. I felt guilty but I kept praying for us. It was winter during this time. I had purchased a larger car so that he would have leg room. He wasn't able to bend his leg yet. He risked his own health rather than let me help him. He walked through the snow, risking permanent damage to his limbs. He was good. He was still the victim. I found myself begging him again. I wanted to help him. I would run after him in the snow begging him to let me help me. He ignored me. I stopped begging. I was hard to see him risk his fragile health. I would drive by him as he walked to the bus stop blocks away from our home. I would try to convince him to let me drive him. He ignored me. I stopped asking. Each time he left the house I prayed that God would heal him in spite of himself.

Cruelty

$\mathcal{I}$had taken a position as staff chaplain at a local hospital about the time my husband came home from the hospital. I worked around his therapy and doctor schedules. The months to follow were more violent but I was also stronger. There were two social workers that helped me walk through the months leading up to our divorce. They knew he was abusive but no one knew the whole story.

I always thought he would go to rehabilitation. I was committed to him. For eight months he deliberately tried to run me out of the house. He had begun walking with crutches around early March of that year. I will always admire him for his determination. Whether he yearned for his lover or he just wanted to get well, he defied all the odds. I was praying for him when he was still bedridden. Along with my prayer that God would help him become drug free, I prayed that he would be well again. My husband's health was getting better but he hadn't changed. In fact, he would treat me crueler than before. How could someone go through such tragedy and not change?

The rules became more stringent. He forgot my name again and added *whore* to the list. His drug friends were calling again. I finally acknowledged our lives were totally separate. He continued to speak highly of me in public and disdain me at home. He stopped using household things. He bought his own towels, bedsheets and comforter. He used his own dishes. He used his own soap. Instead of using the car I bought for his comfort, he bought one just like it but a different color. He even hid his furniture polish from me. I had to buy my own furniture polish. In May of that year I published my first book. I scheduled telephone interviews. He played his music so loud that I could not hear the caller. He insisted that I move my computer out of the third bedroom but I couldn't keep it in his house. One of my friends from work came over for a visit. We were surfing the Internet looking for airlines tickets for she and her husband. He emerged from his bedroom, announced his house wasn't the public library and put her out of the house. I couldn't comb my hair in his bathroom without sweeping and mopping the floor. He didn't want my hair on his floor. I couldn't plant flowers around the patio that spring either. It was his patio. He would park his car so close to my car that I would have to roll over to the driver's side from the passenger's side when I wanted to drive my car. One time when I left my car keys in the door, he removed them and threw them away. I had to have the remote and the keys made over. He laughed about it with one of his co-workers. I wasn't allowed to have exercise equipment in his house. In the middle of the summer, if I opened a window or a door, he would close it shut and hold it there so I could not reopen it. Here was a man who could barely walk but rose up with enough strength to try to destroy me. When mail came addressed to Mr. and Mrs., he would not give it to me. I missed weddings and graduations that year. There were two wedding invitations that I was expecting. Both had come. He refused to let me see them. He told me that I had done nothing worthy of being his wife. He filed income taxes separately but would not tell me what deductions he used. I wasn't allowed to wash my car in the driveway. It was his water and his driveway. One afternoon while he was away, I washed my car anyway! A lady from our church was driving by. She stopped and we began to wash her car too! My husband came home. He announced he did not pay rent, it was his house and there would be no car washing in his driveway. I can still see her driving down the street with suds all over her car. Our kitchen oven needed repairing. The electronic panel malfunctioned. It beeped continually. My husband wouldn't let me get it repaired. I called the repairman anyway. He insulted the repairman at the door. If he wanted the oven repaired he would call a repairman. The oven beeped from September through the end of October. Two of my husband's co-workers came to visit him. He wasn't home. They heard the beeping. I pretended it recently malfunctioned. Several weeks later, they returned for a visit. It was still beeping. I finally told them the truth.

The worst cruelty was his throwing out more of my possessions. This time he added my children's things to the list. In my 22 x 12 feet of area in the basement were my treasures. My little corner space was never as well kept as his basement area. During his illness every thing went down to the basement. By the time he was able to walk downstairs, the basement was a storage room. He was furious. He told me that I had a certain time to clean it up or he would throw everything out. I cleaned up everything except my little space. My office space was messy, as usual. I had sorted out the clothes in the laundry room. I would wash when I got around to it. It wasn't good enough. One afternoon, I had forgotten my money. I went home to get my wallet and noticed a truck in the driveway. I could see my belongings piled high. Years of treasures were piled high on that trash truck. My daughter's award winning art pieces from junior high and high school. There were baby items that should have been handed down to my new grandbaby. My beautiful Wilton cake plates and cake decorating items. My computer, my treadmill, my ab-roller, lamps and a small table that I made with my own hands. My maternal grandmother had died a few years earlier. After I could assess what was missing, my grandma's baking things were gone too. My brownie camera from grade school was gone. My sewing kit and box of material and patterns were gone. The clothing in the laundry room was gone. He simply scooped them up and had them hauled away. I tried to get some of my things back. He wouldn't let me take them off the truck. He did not want my junk in his house. The truth is that I was in a daze. I couldn't find God anymore. Didn't God see what he was doing? If God was really God, why did he let me suffer under my husband's hand? It broke me. I completely gave up. He was delighted at my response. He actually laughed in my face. He laughed. It was unbelievable. Another insult. Insult after insult. Where was God? If God was so powerful and merciful, why couldn't he control my husband? My mind took me back to a time when I had knelt by him as he sat on the sofa in the basement. I was praying for us. When I rose from my knees, he told me that I could pray all I wanted to. "It wasn't going to do me one damn bit of good." It was his house. Was he right? Was he more powerful than God?

I returned to work dazed. My office is across from the social workers. One of them noticed there was something wrong. I guess my face was pale by then. She opened up her arms and I fell into them. I didn't cry. I can't describe how I felt. I remember telling her that my spirit was broken. I felt broken. I told her what he had done. That evening, my neighbor told me that he and a friend watched the trash men load my things on their truck. They watched helplessly as my husband continued his abuse. My neighbor had witnessed my husband's verbal attacks on me several times. Once my neighbor was measuring an area where I wanted a deck built. My husband reminded me that it was his house. A deck would interfere with his satellite dish. I told him that we could move it a few feet away. He cursed me.

While my neighbor was talking I remembered my husband agreeing to replace our worn floor tile with ceramic tile. After weeks of our matching patterns, we decided on the perfect one. My husband wouldn't go shopping with me even in good health. He was confined to the bed during that time, so I would bring tiles to his bedside for his opinion. One of his co-workers came to measure the area. My husband announced there would be no ceramic tile in his house. When was it going to end?

I thought it wasn't too late to retrieve my

treasures. I asked my husband for the name of the trash hauling people. He told me to get out of his room. I cried, I begged and he laughed.

That was a difficult evening. I lost hope. I was afraid. I knocked at my husband's door. He never invited me in his bedroom so I opened the door. "Bitch, close my door." I told him that I was scared. "Scared of what?" "I don't know, I am just scared." He turned over in his bed and told me to close his door. His room had become his refuge instead of the basement. I went to bed that night with many thoughts going through my head. "There really wasn't a God I don't think. If there was a God he has lost his power. Why would he heal my husband enough for him to continue mistreating me? Why did I have to turn the other cheek while my husband enjoyed emotionally slapping me with each turn? Is there a cap on this forgiveness thing? How much was enough? Was I eventually going to end up dead? Why was I still there? Why should I have to leave my home?" I resented my husband. If it had not been for me, he would still be living in his one bedroom apartment with nothing. He had only cut the grass twice since we lived in the house but wouldn't let me cut it without asking his permission. Our house looked unkempt but he criticized my housekeeping? He never cleaned except to humiliate me. "There couldn't be a God." I lay there with thoughts coming quickly. My mind said, "Just renounce God. Your husband is more powerful than he is anyway." It was around 3 AM. I called a pastor friend of mine in another city. As soon as he answered the phone I wept. I wept and wept. I couldn't talk. After

I composed myself, I told him what my husband did. He urged me to leave him right away for my own safety. How much more did he have to do for me to leave? That was a good question. The next day was my scheduled CPE class. I went in a daze. For anyone who has taken CPE, it is not always the best arena to tread when you are already hurting. I wouldn't talk. I sat there fighting back the tears. I did well. I thought I was okay.

When I arrived home he was his usual self. He was on the telephone talking so joyously about his day. He had a wonderful day. He had visited with some friends. . . on and on he went. He was in a very good mood. I stayed in my room most of the evening trying to fall asleep. I couldn't sleep. The voices came back. They were stronger this time. "God really did not exist at all. That was why everything had happened to me. You see, God knew that my husband was more powerful than he was. God wasn't real, I was the one who didn't know that God wasn't real. All of my work for God had been a waste of time. I was stuck with my husband." I had taken those vows. He had broken every vow and smashed them several times in my face. It was a reasonable answer for everything that happened to me. All I had to do was open my mouth and confess that there really is no God.

I wouldn't do it. I gritted my teeth. I wouldn't do it. I fell to the floor prostrate. At that moment I remembered the visit. Years earlier, the Lord appeared to me in that very room. My face was to the floor, my eyes were tightly closed but I could see him again. He said nothing on his visit. I saw him.

He was clothed in the most beautiful white garment I have ever seen. He was so holy and loving. I remembered when I first felt his presence. It had been a few years but I still remembered. When I awakened from my sleep that night, I knew he was there. I couldn't look at him. I was ashamed of my flesh. I was so mortal. The filthiness of my flesh stood in the way of my Savior and me. I slid out of the bed. I lay prostrate on the floor. I looked up only for a moment. Then I saw him. He gave me something that night. I know he did. I never knew what it was. Suddenly, that very moment, I knew what it was! He gave me himself! He knew this night was coming. He saw my husband when he threw out my treasures. He saw how I was suffering! My broken state was now in his hands.

No, I would not bow down to satan. I began to call on the name of my Jesus. First it was hard to speak. I began softly. I was so weak. But as I called on him, he began to strengthen me. I lifted my face from the floor sobbing. God is real, he is more powerful than my husband. Then I remembered The Book of Job. I remembered the conversation between God and satan about Job. Was God considering me as faithful as Job? My experience hadn't been anything like Job's. Was this my Job experience? Could it be that God was letting me see what I was made of? I wish he had chosen another route but it made sense. Did I have some inner strength that I did not know about? I began to rebuke satan. He would not have me. I did not belong to him, I belonged to God. I am God's child! I began to praise God with a loud voice. I rose to my knees and raised my hands to heaven. I blessed the Lord and thanked him for my salvation. He lifted my head! Revival had come. As I blessed the Lord, the Holy Spirit was bringing scriptures back to my remembrance that would affirm me. I was strengthened by almighty God! My tears kept coming but they were tears of assurance now. God is real. I knew God had been with me all the time. I didn't have all the answers but I knew he was real. It seemed that the whole neighborhood could hear me shouting and praising God. My husband could not stand the victory. He got up and left the house. It was around 3 AM. I praised God for hours. I shouted for victory. The battle was not mine. It was the Lord's.

The next few days were interesting. My husband seldom kept his bedroom door open. I was working on my computer in the bedroom across the hallway. I heard him on the telephone. He was telling someone that he would pick up the truck the next morning and move the rest of my things. My heart sank. What more was he going to throw out? I began to cry. Then I stopped. I wasn't going to cry anymore. I made up my mind that hell would freeze before he threw anymore of my possessions away. That afternoon I called my attorney. She wrote a letter to him advising that he would be taken to court to explain his actions. The house was marital property and we shared equally in its use. The letter was mailed the same afternoon.

I did not go to work that next morning. I stayed right there. I was working on my computer. He slightly opened his door. I heard him tell someone that he was going to get the truck. They would move all of my things at 10:00 that morning. He left right after the conversation. I sneaked into his room and pushed redial. He had called the time. He was harassing me. Was he purposely harassing me? Why? I was good to him. Why was he doing this to me? It didn't matter. I waited for him and anyone to show up. Neither my possessions nor I would be moved that day.

The letter from my attorney arrived later that afternoon. He read it, called her a bitch and announced that no one told him what to do in his house. I tried to explain to him that our house was marital property. I had the same rights that he had. He could not continue to throw out my things. I never told him I knew he was harassing me purposely. I was beginning to understand why God tells us to watch, pray and keep our mouths shut. The enemy doesn't need to know what your next move will be. For that matter, I did not know what my next move would be. I was trying to survive. I had five more months to endure before my husband would file for divorce.

After this experience, my prayers began to change. I wanted the pain to go away. I wanted my husband gone. I had been praying that God would heal our marriage, help him get off of drugs and just make everything perfect. I still wanted him to be free from drugs, but equally wanted all of the abuse, the madness and the humiliation to stop. I no longer cared how God did it. I was tired of crying. I was tired of being tired. My friends wouldn't come near the house or call. He put my teenaged niece and nephew out of our house. He would be rude to them on the telephone. He began using derogatory names when referring to my mother and sister. When he attended church, he would speak to everyone but me. When someone joins the congregation for membership, it is customary that we all welcome them. My husband would join the welcome line and not shake my hand. He mistreated me at home and now church. I felt trapped. My role as one of the pastors left me defenseless. I couldn't say or do anything. He humiliated me at church too. I wanted it all to stop.

Each day I prayed that God would help me see and not see, hear and not hear. Many knew how he was treating me, they were urging me to leave him, some just gave up on me. It was confusing. I didn't know what to do. The Book of James says that when we lack wisdom we can ask God. He will help us. So I did. Each day I prayed that God would keep me safe, continue to heal my broken spirit and do whatever he thought was necessary for me to have peace again. I was no longer walking in my own strength. I was too spiritually broken to do anything. I was depending solely on God's mercy. I asked God to pick me up in his arms. However God worked it out, it was fine with me. I couldn't make it on my own anymore.

The months following continued to be full of name calling and demands. He added more rules. I shed more tears but I was no longer expecting behavioral changes from him. I was depending solely on God. When I found myself reasoning with him, I would stop. I would find a quiet space and pray for myself. My prayer was simple, "Lord please help me."

The World Trade Center's twin towers had been hit by airplanes that morning. I was sitting in a patient's room. Her daughter was working in that tower. It was a horrific time for everyone in America. I was scared too. What did it all mean? My daughter and sons phoned me. They were afraid. I called my husband. I told him I was scared. Were we at war now? Did all this mean that more violence would happen? He hung up on me. Not even a tragedy of this magnitude would soften his heart of steel. He seemed undaunted by the events of the week.

He was his usual demanding self for the next few days. I had just purchased an exerciser for my mid-section and set it up in the family room. He gave me 8 hours to tear it down and get it out of his house. His house was not the gym. I took the equipment back to the store to keep peace. I decided to use my exercise videos. Then he added that I couldn't do my kick boxing to his list of rules. I ignored him. I popped in the video and began my routine. He was still recuperating and walked with great difficulty. He held on to the walls until he made it into the family room. I heard him coming but I continued my routine. He almost lost his balance, but he turned off the TV. I could not use the VCR or the TV in his house. Not a problem for me. I went downstairs. I would finish exercising down there. He managed to get down the basement stairs. He unplugged my new treadmill and told me to get all of my exercise equipment out of his house by noon or it went into the trash. I fell apart. When was it going to end? I called the police. I couldn't stop crying. They sent out a police car. The officers parked down the street and walked up to the house. I was on the front step crying. They were very nice, very consoling. We had a good conversation. My husband came out of the side door and got in his car. He was backing out of the driveway when an officer stopped him. My husband told them that we simply had a misunderstanding. All was well. There was no problem at all. I was just overreacting to a disagreement. He was good. He was a typical abuser. He was also a coward. I pulled myself together and went into work. When I came home, he was furious. How dare I call the police on him! He added even more descriptive words to the threats and names he was already calling me.

All over the world, prayers were going out for the families of the 9/11 dead and missing. Our congregation was no exception. Sunday after the towers fell, I was getting ready to go to the prayer service for those who where missing or dead and their loved ones. My husband was on another rampage. I was curling my hair in the bedroom since I wasn't allowed to fix my hair in the bathroom without sweeping and mopping the floor. My husband did not want my hair on his floor. He had just finished calling me whores and bitches. I was crying. As I looked in the mirror trying to finish my hair, I saw myself. I was a wreck. I also envisioned the planes flying into the World Trade Center's twin towers. My husband was no different than the terrorists. It was as though my tears went back into their tear ducts. I stopped crying, put my curling iron down and kicked in my husband's door. In response to his usual, "Bitch, get out of my room", I informed him that I was not his bitch or his whore. I was the righteousness of God in Christ Jesus. I informed him that it was my house too and I would no longer be abiding by his rules. Whether I lived or died would remain to be seen but I would not die with his feet on me. I was careful but I wasn't his doormat any longer. When he cursed me, I quickly rebuked him and satan in the name of Jesus. When he threatened me, I pleaded the blood of Jesus over my life and told him that God would fight him for me. I was still afraid to leave home for fear of his throwing out my things. I would not continue to live in fear! I booked two trips! I went to see the Lion King in Toronto. I asked him not to bother my things while I was gone. He assured me that they would be gone. I told him that I would rather he not throw out my things but if he did, I'd see him in court. A few weeks later I went to New Orleans. He threatened me again. No problem, the courts had openings on the dockets and I would eventually book one. I was not going to live my life in fear any longer.

While I was in New Orleans, he filed for divorce. One week later, he had the hospital operator page me overhead. When I picked up the phone he informed me that he had filed for divorce. He wanted to know where I wanted the papers sent to me. I was devastated. There would be no rehabilitation or reconciliation. I picked up the divorce papers from his attorney. I asked why my husband was divorcing me. His attorney told me that I had three options. One of those options was to try and work things out with my husband. I tried. I asked him why he was divorcing me. He cursed me out. After all I had put up with, it was for naught. He never intended to do anything other than what he had already done. All those years of abuse and humiliation, for what? The next morning I was coming out of my bedroom, he brushed by me. I walked into the bathroom and fell into the bathtub. I cried out to God and asked him to help me. I heard my husband laughing at me.

His laughter stopped my tears. I went to the kitchen. As I was reaching for the refrigerator door, my mind took me back to King David's and Bathseba's baby. I could hear King David's servant ask him why he was no longer grieving. His baby had just died. Instead of continuing to lament, he told is servant "while the baby was alive I fasted and I wept. Who knows? The Lord might be gracious and let the child live. Now he is dead. Why should I fast? I can go to him, but he cannot return to me." (2 Samuel 12:20-23). It was over. The Lord told me to go on with my life. He would handle my husband; his arms were not too short.

I never spoke to him again about the divorce. I hired my attorney to represent me. Six months later we were divorced. During that time, the court had to intervene a few times. He always played his music loud. I had been wearing ear plugs for nearly a year so that I could sleep when he felt the need to blast me out of the house. My grandson found my earplugs on my dresser. He asked his grandpa what they were for. The music got louder. I moved to the basement. He moved his speakers to the family room and opened the basement door. I asked him to turn down the music, he turned it up even louder. I called the police and asked if someone would at least drive by our house. If they could hear the music, could they at least knock on the door and ask that he turn it down? They did. The next day I was turning in for the evening. He barely made it down the basement steps. I could hear him breathing as he carefully took each step holding on to the rail. He washed clean clothes with all of the lights on to keep me awake. I prayed myself to sleep. Then next day I settled down in my new basement home. I reached for the telephone. He had taken the telephone. I went out and purchased another telephone. Then next evening when I got ready for bed, my blankets were missing. I went upstairs and took the bedding from my room. The next morning I phoned my attorney. The court intervened and the harassment stopped.

It was close to Thanksgiving. My daughter was getting engaged! Obviously her future husband had to meet my approval first. I was thrilled for them. I was going to meet my new son. She was afraid to bring him home. She hadn't been to the house since my husband threw her out almost two years before. I assured her that all would be well. We would have a nice Thanksgiving. She would not be humiliated in front of her company. I called my attorney. I asked that she let my husband know, through his attorney, that my children would be home for Thanksgiving dinner. Since he only spent one Thanksgiving with us the entire time we were married, it should pose no problem. He informed his attorney that if my children showed up for Thanksgiving dinner, it would be unpleasant for them. Those words hurt. My children had always respected him. His own children had not celebrated his birthday or father's day. Even after we learned he mistreated us for his crack-cocaine habit we never forgot important days for him. After his accident, my children sent him flowers and get well cards. They remembered him for Christmas. They didn't deserve his harshness.

A few days before Thanksgiving, I began preparing for my Thanksgiving meal. I think I cooked enough food and baked enough sweets to feed our entire neighborhood. I would not be a prisoner in my own home. My children would come home whenever they needed to. It was a pleasant Thanksgiving. He left early and stayed late. We were used to it. We weren't expecting him. I was still hurting, but I was no longer looking out of the window wondering where he was. I was no longer keeping his food warm for him. We spent only one New Year's together. This would be the first New Year's Eve that I would not cry while he was either with his friends or enjoying his music in the basement. I was too ashamed to attend Watch Night Service at church for fear someone would ask where my husband was. Unbeknown to me, my husband celebrated his New Years with his crack-cocaine.

My husband thought that he could simply erase me. I knew he was struggling. He had his own health issues. He worsened his health when he punished me for standing up for myself. He wouldn't let me help him when he genuinely needed it. His self-defeating behavior continued as the divorce moved forward. He wouldn't answer questions for discovery. He thought it would be a fair property settlement for me to keep the house I purchased when I was 19. He would keep the marital property.

I would not be entitled to any of our marital assets since I had my own money and was working. The courts had to intervene for him to complete the appropriate forms. He would not compromise, he owed me nothing.

Our attorneys scheduled a date for mediation. I asked that all of our assets be divided equally or, as the mediator deemed fair and equitable. My husband detailed exactly what property he wanted which included our house. I was willing to give my husband the house if he would give me my portion of the equity. He refused. He wasn't willing to give me anything. My name was not on the house. I had been sick when he closed on the property. He thought I was not entitled to any portion of the house. He told the mediator and our attorneys, "I'm not giving her a dime." He never regarded our home as mine. Since I was willing to share all of my assets including my rental property, the settlement reflected a fair property settlement. When it was all said and done, he had lost everything he tried so hard to take from me including the house. I tried to give him more. His attorney reminded us that he had written down what he wanted. It was much less than what I was trying to give him. He received exactly what he asked for going into the mediation minus our house. He was angry throughout the proceedings, he degraded me in front of the mediator and our attorneys. My husband paid a high price to nurse his lover. He valued crack-cocaine more than our marriage. He decided our wedding vows were of no consequence to him and his lover. His addiction and abuse had no limits. For years he walked all over me and mine. He used our wedding vows against me. He ignored my tears. He enjoyed my pain. He mocked my prayers. I am so thankful that God was listening. Perhaps God was waiting for me to get from under his feet. I will never know it all, but that day I was delivered from my husband's cruelty and crack-cocaine.

I gave my husband six weeks to find another home. I also kept him on my medical insurance until he got his own health insurance. When I returned home from mediation, I could actually park in the garage and open the driver's side of my car. My husband had left room. It was the spring of the year. I didn't go in the house. I went to a flower shop. I bought a lovely plant. I went home, walked on the patio with plant in hand and cried. I set my plant on the patio. I was free.

I walked into the back yard. I felt like Abraham. All I could see was mine. I walked from each end of the lot to the other end. It was all mine. I could plant as many flowers as I wanted! My mind went back to the day he had my basement treasures taken away. He also threw out my flower pots and patio furniture. My garden tools were in the shed, they were thrown out too. He couldn't throw out my things anymore! He wasn't willing to share in the upkeep of the property, he simply ruled it. I could cut the grass, I was free! I could wash down the siding on the house. He hadn't allowed me to use his water. The house really needed a bath. I was free! I shouted from one end of the property to the next. I got my cell phone out of my purse, I called my friends. They could come over now! I was free! Still, it was a sad day. My marriage was over. The vows that we had taken meant nothing to him. Had he always meant to use me? Maybe I will always hold on to the thought that he tried but his addiction got the best of him. I will never know. The important thing is that I survived and I am free now. I missed him for a long time. The one thing I held on to was my perfect wedding. It was the happiest day of my life when I married my husband. Our church was full of friends and family. We were thrilled. That never changed for me even after the divorce. How could he leave after I tried so hard to make things work? I am glad he left. Dreams and memories are good. They help you when you have nothing else.

I stayed in the basement for almost a month after he left. Finally, my dear friend reminded me that I could move upstairs. The house was mine.

Reconciliation

     Since finding my former husband's drugs and paraphernalia, I have prayed every day that he would be drug free some day. It had been over two years since he left. I was making great progress. Oh how I enjoyed life! I was safe at home and safe at church! I remember how I used to cling to the altar feeling safe, knowing my husband couldn't hurt me there. He stopped attending our church. Those days were behind me.

     The Lord has tremendously blessed me. Every once in a while I remember those times that I was so upset I actually couldn't remember where I was supposed to be. Down the highway I would go, lamenting and crying out to God for help. I remember the morning that I asked to drive his car to another city. I was scheduled to teach Bible courses all day. My car wasn't working properly. He wouldn't let me drive his car. I was so hurt. He gave his old car to a co-worker, but I couldn't drive his car. I was paying the installments for him. I drove to the wrong city. My car broke down. Those days were behind me.

     After a lengthy absence, my former husband began coming back to church. We have two services. I always attend the early service. The more he came the more I began to remember little bits and pieces I had once forgotten. This posed no problem. He began attending the second service. I was glad. I would only see him in passing. All was well again. I shared with a pastor friend that he had come back to church. I was uneasy. I always welcomed people back to church when they had been absent awhile. I hadn't planned on doing that for my former husband. He had humiliated me enough at church. I stayed clear of him. After some time, he actually spoke to me. His great niece was with him that morning. For the first time in over four years, he spoke a civil word to me! It was so foreign to me, I didn't know what to do. Finally, I thought it unwise to make exceptions. It is my duty as a shepherd. At the prompting of my pastor friend, I went out of my way to welcome him back and assure him all had been forgiven. Before I could reach out to him, I would write scripts, practicing what I needed to say to him. My pastor friend helped me to talk out my fears. Though I could never be sure of what he might do to me, I concluded he was trying. I welcomed him. He even began attending Sunday School and Bible Study. I made sure that he received his Sunday School Commentary along with the other adult students. It reminded me of when he was able to walk again from his accident. I was proud of him. Besides, life was good. I had just celebrated my 50th birthday. I remembered how I cried when years before, he gave me a clown card for my birthday. Our former wedding anniversary had just past. I remembered the last anniversary gift I gave him - a Kenneth Cole watch – he threw it in the trash. I remembered it on his birthday. Time heals all wounds. I wished him a happy birthday one Saturday during a social at church. I even offered to take him to lunch or dinner for his birthday. I was facing my fears. He couldn't hurt me anymore. It felt good. I was on the mend. Yes, there is room for everyone at the cross! He had his service and I had mine.

The next day, it was our usual early morning service. We were singing the opening hymn. I looked up and saw him coming into the sanctuary. It was strange; he didn't attend early morning service. He did this morning. He was accompanied by a woman. They sat so close that they overlapped. They came and they went. In less than one minute, the only decent thing I had left of our marriage was gone. The memories of my perfect wedding no longer existed. It was all gone. He used the only place I felt safe to hurt me again. He took away my only good memory. He knew I would suffer quietly, I always had.

When I found his drugs, it was hard to breathe. When I realized that he intentionally hurt me just because he could, I couldn't breathe. The Amtrak did not roll over me. It sat on me. Every thing in my body hurt. Nothing was spared. It was all gone. The pain, the rejection, the ridicule, the abuse, it was all for naught. He made a mockery of my kindness again. All those times he had criticized our congregation continued to play over and over in my mind. Why was it so important that he attend a service that I attended? He comes back to the only place I could find refuge from him? He had to swing at me again. It worked. It was final examination time. Am I really a shepherd? Would I be like the shepherds who sought to destroy Israel? God saw them you know. He peeked at them and saw the intentions of their hearts. He even showed them to Ezekiel (34:8-10). Would I go down in history as a good shepherd or one that was going to destroy this sheep? I was leaning towards destruction. He robbed me of a marriage and now he opens the wound and pours a zillion tons of salt in it? I wanted to destroy him. Then I realized that he really couldn't hurt me anymore. My life was so much better without him. Yet, it was so painful. I had to fight the voices. Each time satan reminded me of the hell I went through with him, I remembered that Calvary included my former husband. Each time I thought about those times he humiliated me and put my family out of the house, I thanked God that we were all safe now. Each time I thought about the humiliation of a going through a divorce I did not want, I thought of how blessed I am because he left. I am truly blessed. Church is the one place a person should be able to come and find solace. I did. I am a shepherd. All things are no longer equal. My former husband is a sheep. I came so close to hating him when I learned he sacrificed me and our marriage for his crack-cocaine. God not only saw the shepherds, he also saw the sheep. Is our church large enough for me to grieve? I think so. Years of praying and holding my peace have transformed my heart and behavior. I do not want to destroy him or anyone else for that matter. I made up my mind that I would continue treating him with the love of Christ. There is room at the cross for everyone.

But what about the pain? Deliverance doesn't necessarily mean that we are pain free. Soon, my former husband asked our pastor (and my colleague) to marry him and his friend. The painful memories of how he treated me could not be contained. What about my wedding vows? Is his god so lenient that my vows meant nothing? Why would he ask our pastor to marry them? My former husband's father is a pastor. Her father is a pastor with a lovely church in the same city. Why, of all places, the only place I felt secure from him? Why get married in our church? Her father has a church. His father has a church. It was as though it were yesterday. My security was gone. My refuge had been snatched away from me. I had nothing left. My perfect wedding was gone. The only decent memory I had was gone. I cried and wept. However, this time I was not alone. My friends knew I was in pain, they found me. They consoled me.

One of our ministers who was experiencing temporary health problems asked that I assume her duties in the second worship service. One morning while leading the Decalogue I glanced among the congregation. My former husband was talking to his fiancée. When I saw this, my mind took me back to the many times that I begged him to talk with me. He usually shooed me away with his arm. One time he took his foot and kicked me out of his way like I was a piece of trash. Unbeknown to me, he continued to enjoy his high while listening to his music. I had not thought about that day for years. I remember it well. It was too painful then, I can grieve now. This time I am not alone. It was too humiliating to share with anyone then. How could I admit that the man I loved and cherished treated me like I was trash?

I was able to get through the worship service with little difficulty. It was when I was alone that the pain was wrenching. I allowed myself to give in to the pain. I wailed and I wept. I also called my pastor. His wife answered the phone. She heard my pain. She gave me comfort and support. She told me that she loved me. I was no longer alone. My pastor listened as I continued to cry out. What about my vows? Didn't anyone care? I kept them. I cherished them. Why did all this pain have to come back? It was too much. I couldn't relive the pain. I wanted to run. I wanted to leave. I wanted to come out of myself. My pastor shepherded me. He promised he would walk with me. This time I would not be alone.

God allows us to feel the pain so that he can heal us. I wasn't able to digest all of the pain then, the suffering would have been too much for me to bear. I am stronger now.

My former husband's return forced me to revisit many painful, dormant memories. God has given us a wonderfully complex body and mind. He lets us heal a little bit at a time. He has fixed it so that our minds will only let us remember and feel so much pain. When we are stronger, he heals us a little more. He lets the dormant memories remind us that we need more of his healing balm.

My dormant memories were even more painful since my former husband has shown no remorse for the pain that he caused my family and me. He has now invaded the space I once found secure. I'm not able to avoid the pain any longer. My loss was significant. My dreams were shattered. My person was devalued. He made a mockery of our commitment to God and one another. We cannot avoid grief. We all grieve when something meaningful has been taken from us.

Now I begin my grief work. As I work through my complex feelings, I know God is with me. Though my former husband still treats me with disdain, God loves me. I am no longer isolated in my despair. This time the humiliation and pain will not make me feel as though I am abandoned. There comes a time in our lives when we must not let our abusers hold us captive. I am facing my pain. There are blessings behind me. There are blessings ahead of me. My space will remain sacred. God's house is spacious. There is room for my abuser. This time is different. I know that I am loved. I know that I am valued. Perhaps his being here is part of my healing. God doesn't need him to be absent in order to make me whole. As I cried out to God, I realized that many of us will have to do our grief work in the presence of our abuser particularly when there are children involved.

Our grandson often attends church with me. He was also a victim of my former husband's addiction. He has spent a significant part of his life with us. He practically lived with us since birth. His parents had been gracious with letting us keep him until he started kindergarten. After that we had him every weekend and often most of the week. A few weeks after my husband threw out my basement treasures and back yard items, he threw out some of our grandson's toys. Our neighbor had given our grandson an original Big Wheel. His son had it when he was a toddler. Now that was a true treasure! His pretend uncle gave him something pretty special. We also went to garage sales. Only a true garage sale person knows the treasures that await you from the attics of others. My grandson had been afraid of his grandpa for some time. Grandpa would often spank him and hit him harder when he cried. I stopped leaving him with my husband a few years before the divorce. We had to think of a place where grandpa wouldn't find our treasures. We were careful to find a place out of his reach. The outside shed. What better place? It was a reasonable assumption. He had already thrown out my things in it. Since he didn't do yard work, anything was safe beyond the patio. That was just the right place. He would not return there. Wrong. He found our treasures and threw them out too. Nothing was spared from his wrath, not even our grandson's toys. I will always remember those big tears streaming down his face when he discovered that his grandpa had thrown away his toys too. His little heart ached. He had why questions too. "Why would Poppee throw away my toys? I have never done anything to him."

Listening to his pain was hard. His grandpa was in the other room. Our grandson's tears did not move him at all. I asked our grandson what would make him feel better. He said that we needed to move away from Poppee so that he couldn't be mean to us anymore. We said a prayer that day. We asked God to make grandpa stop being so mean or make him find another place to live. The divorce did not heal the painful memories. It simply gave us some space to begin the process. We have discussed that he doesn't have to be around grandpa if he still hurts. God won't mind at all. There is lots of room at church for all of us. This has been a teachable moment for my grandson. His unfortunate ordeal with his grandpa helped him learn that God has a way of making things better, even when we hurt. We wrote a story about his dog. Her name is Nala. Nala went to visit Grandma after Poppee left her. She was sad and alone. Nala saw how sad she was. Nala cheered Grandma up. Grandma smiled again! Nala moved in with Grandma. Now they are both much happier. *My Grandma's Dog* was published in October 2004. My grandson narrates the story about Nala and me. It is for all who need a little more joy.

Grandpa never apologized to our grandson. Perhaps a love story that begins with grief and ends with joy will help others find a bit more joy and hope. It certainly helped my grandson find some peace in the midst of his Poppee's cruelty.

Addiction

Addiction of any kind is a demonic spirit emanating straight from the pits of hell. It is one of satan's schemes to destroy God's people. We are God's image bearers. Regardless of the color of our eyes, hair and/or skin, we all belong to God. Mankind was not designed to be destructive and selfish. It was after Adam and Eve disobeyed God's instructions that demonic forces became a part of the human condition. The fruit from the tree of the knowledge of good and evil bore the resources to all of life's possibilities. Unfortunately, those resources included evil. Our all wise Creator knew his once perfect and innocent couple could no longer remain in their blissful Eden. There was another tree in Eden, the tree of life. Should they reach out their hand and eat of that tree in their present state, they would be damned to an eternal existence, struggling between good and evil. They would have no recourse to overcome satan's constant attack against them. Their offspring would face the same dilemma.

Barred from living forever, satan began manufacturing any means necessary to kill our knowledge of God's love and commitment. Pain and suffering often overshadow those good feelings we associate with a loving God. Can God exist when there is pain and suffering? If he exists, where is he? Addictive demons only focus is to cause pain and suffering for its victim and those who become co-dependent with them. The addictive demonic spirit sucks the life out of people. It is so powerful that it becomes their god. Addictive demons only care about themselves.

Unlike a loving and protective God, addictive demons attack the very fiber and being of their victims. Addiction takes control of their victim's mind. Our body and mind function together. Mental illness, physical infirmities – they are the result of satan's schemes to destroy our relationship with God. If physical deformities were meant to be another expression of God's image, satan's scheme has now deemed it as abnormal and unacceptable. We put those with mental illness in institutions. We shut away those whose physical conditions were not acceptable to the greater society. The greater society condemns the poor and unfortunate, often blaming the victim.

Addiction is different. The character of addiction is a carefully designed demonic plan. Satan has created a living force that awakens the secret places in our minds. Satan has to begin with our mind to truly possess us. God designed us, body and mind. We can also add our soul. Dependent upon your view of body and soul; our mind, soul and body work interdependently. Our soul is the essence of what is important to us. Mind and soul can be used interchangeably. However you wish to use these terms, addiction possesses both. Our mind tells our body what it needs to do. I doubt that the design of our mind was altered when evil became a part of the human condition, however, satan began to have access to our sound minds. He began to invade those secret places once reserved for God. Those pleasure centers were meant to praise God and see the beauty of his creation. The pleasure center was reserved for those special times. The addictive demonic spirit grabs hold of the pleasure center of the victim's mind. The victim is always trying to satisfy the secret place once reserved for those special moments in life. The victim ultimately gives him or herself over to the addictive demonic spirit's master, satan himself.

Addictive demonic spirits look for opportunities to destroy people. This happens in a number of ways. As children we might be exposed to lewd and vile behavior of adults. Those spirits are just waiting for fresh new souls to destroy. Parents and caregivers should be nurturing and laying the foundation to overcome the challenges that our fallen human condition might bring. Instead they expose young minds to too much adult information. Immature minds see activities without the benefit of knowing how to weigh the consequences. They model behavior in innocence. Generational addiction and self-defeating behavior is a carefully planned scheme of satan. Families and communities are destroyed with ease.

Both our words and actions can create deep voids in our children. "You will never be anything." "You are just like your father." Can you imagine how this impacts a tender heart when they feel their father or mother isn't kind or responsible? The addictive demonic spirit offers a better solution to their hurting heart.

As I watch the anti-drug commercials, I smile.

Parents or those responsible to rear the child are the best anti-drug. We need to know what our children are doing and where they are going. Neglecting our children exposes them to some of the same dangers as child abuse. When we fail to care for our children, we leave them vulnerable to satan's schemes. They have no direction or protection. Addictive demonic spirits look for children who are open to the slightest appearance of security and acceptance. They simply want to belong. No one is exempt from satan's schemes.

Addictive demonic spirits also look for people like me. All of the signs of my former husband's drug addiction were in my face. Was I too stupid to see them? I had stereotyped what a drug addict looked like. He was neat and ordered. He was uniformily dressed for work. His position was one of status. I never saw the other side of his life. I also thought I was above being abused. I had fought too hard to let anything destroy my dignity and integrity. Satan knew that I would endure just about anything to be able to hold my head up. My wedding vows were the one thing addiction knew I would hold on to. Our marriage never stood a chance. My husband was already married to his crack-cocaine. Addictive demonic spirits look for people like me, "Look! she's the one. Look at the way she carries herself. She is independent and proud. She will not be a burden at all. Two incomes are much better than one. Even better, she will forgive seven times seventy. She teaches the Bible. She won't go against that for better or for worse thing. We have some good years ahead of us with her. She will never tell how we will treat her. She's too proud. Besides, she doesn't know a thing about drug addicts. She's one of those people who thinks she's above us. By the time she figures us out, she'll be one of us."

I often wonder what I would have done if I had known of my former husband's addiction early in our marriage? Would I have succumbed to addiction myself? Did I have the courage to leave him? My relationship with God was shaken because of my husband's cruelty towards me. I worked hard to became strong in the Lord again. It took me years to find my way back to a healthy life. Early on, I wondered if I made a mistake when I married him. It certainly looks as though I did. He even stole my perfect wedding day from me. Whatever the case may have been, our marriage was doomed from the beginning. I would like to think that he was sincere when he proposed. God knows he was romantic! He said all the right words and had all of the right answers. I am no longer in denial. The facts speak for themselves.

After I spoke with my father-in-law, I also researched his behavior with his former wife. Under the Freedom of Information Act, I obtained copies of their divorce information. After reading the information, I knew I was dealing with an experienced abuser. Aside from the physical abuse which she suffered, her story could be my own. Addictive demonic spirits do not discriminate. Often we competent, proud, type A personalities think that we can change a person's behavior. Thinking he was bipolar, I simply made adjustments to deal with the mood disorder. . over and over and over.

I cannot imagine that anyone would stay with a person knowing they are addicted to drugs. On second thought, maybe I can. The hope that someday my husband would get help carried me from insult to humiliation and into an abusive living situation. Telling my story has not been easy. I put up with far too much under the assumption that he loved me, BUT. . .

Abusers do not love. They control. The nature of love nurtures the comfort and health of the person being loved. Abuse is another scheme of satan. It thrilled my former husband to see me beg and cry for his mercy. I was worshipping his god. When I justified everything he did, it made me feel better. It made my hell more palatable.

The addictive demonic spirit knew I would be a good co-dependent victim. It watched me for a while. It watched me attend to prisoners. I took time with them when others would not. I fought for their rights when I thought other staff were a bit too stern with them for their offense. It knew I was strong in faith, I would never give up on my husband.

While I was clinging to my wedding vows, the addictive demonic spirit continued to court the pleasure center of my husband's mind. The mind is our memory base. If you were to ask a drug addict about family details, he wouldn't be able to tell you. When my husband filed for divorce, he wasn't able to give my correct name to his attorney. He never knew that my last name was not hyphenated. I had taken his name and he never even knew it. There is no room for addiction and family. It takes over the mind. The pleasure center is always looking to match that first high. The mind becomes incapable of anything else. It can no longer love anyone else. It has no patience for something that cannot tickle its pleasure zone. Our mind helps us plan our next move. It lets us see our future. It helps us to dream! "A mind is a terrible thing to waste." This is exactly what the addictive demonic spirit does with the mind. The mind is no longer interested in the mundane things of life. Who needs to make love to a woman? The mind needs to nurse the pleasure zone. When I learned my former husband preferred X-rated movies to me, it was a low blow. How could he sit in the basement alone and watch strangers having sex? He wasn't alone. He and his addiction were making love while I was alone. A human being will never satisfy that area of the brain. Crack-cocaine is said to deliver an intensity of pleasure completely outside of the normal range of human experience. It is reported to give a *wonderful state of consciousness* and *makes one feel alive*. Some crack users say it is a *whole body orgasm*. When I learned this, it helped me to understand why my husband had no desire for me as a woman. All energy is spent trying to satisfy the god of addiction. It is a false sense of completeness. Addiction is never satisfied.

Crack and cocaine are dopaminergic drugs. Some drugs release the chemical, serotonin which typically promotes empathy and trust. The victim might be able to maintain some sociability. Crack, cocaine and amphetamines have the reverse effect. It releases a chemical that makes the victim selfish, irritable and suspicious. It's no wonder that my husband made the basement a shrine and treated me less than human.

Crack-cocaine is one of the most selfish and destructive devices of satan. Crack is the highly addictive form of cocaine. When I was researching the effects that crack-cocaine had on my husband, I was astounded. One article emphasized that there was only one ideal time to use crack-cocaine. There was a time in history when doctors would administer the terminally ill cancer patient an elixir known as the "Brompton cocktail". It was reported that not only the patient was thrilled with its gratifying result. The family of the recipient was relieved when they saw *the new-found look of spiritual peace and happiness suffusing the features of a loved one as he(she) prepared to meet his or her Maker.*

There is no acceptable time to use crack and cocaine or any other drug that will interfere with one's ability to be a responsible adult.

Reflections

I wish I could talk about rehabilitation. Unfortunately, it was not part of my own personal experience. I am learning to live with my loss without remorse from my former husband. All was not lost. One of the blessings of prison life and my relationship with my husband was acquiring the skills and grace to work with people in recovery. I had facilitated the substance abuse program at the prison. It was an experience. There was a grouped call SIR (Survivors in Recovery). I thought it was noble that people were actually survivors. What I did not know was that I would also hear the gruesome details of how some of these men raped their children and other young people. They brought out the worst in me. How could I help them? They had no right to hurt innocent children. They deserved to be in prison.

I remember one prisoner who was an older gentleman. He was very polite. He had an adult relationship with his young teenaged daughter. Most of the men I encountered were polite. They weren't at all the way I had anticipated. I guess I should tell you that the night before I was to begin working at a prison, I was extremely nervous. All of sudden, my mangled, raped and suffering body flashed before me. Satan was and continues to be a liar. I crawled onto my bed in a sort of fetal position. Before I could blink, I felt the presence of an angel from God. The angel assured me that I would always be safe. I was to obey the prison rules and God. Knowing I would always be safe, I began my new career in prison.

Getting back to recovery, the stories were a bit overwhelming. What was I to do? Would I conform and become like some prison staff (including chaplains) and degrade the men? Would I simply condemn them to hell and hopelessness? As I listened to their stories, it was pretty apparent that they had already lived in hell and hope was not in abundance. Wouldn't you know it, I was the one who needed to change. Each morning before group, I would get on my knees and ask God to give me his love for the men. After several weeks had passed I began the group without praying first. To my pleasant surprise, God gave me just what I needed to listen and offer them forgiveness and a bit of God's love which most had not experienced. God gave me more of his grace.

This was only the beginning of my shepherd's heart. I learned to pray for men as I smelled the background of feces smeared on the walls of their cells. I also learned how much God loved those we deem unlovable. I met one young man in the hole at the first prison where I worked. The conditions weren't the best. The building was quite aged. It was drafty and damp. The young man could not recuperate from pneumonia. He also had asthma. He could have been my son. I prayed that God would give him better living conditions and help him to get well.

I had already transferred to the second prison. I was making rounds one morning. In the unit I heard a young voice, "Ms. Reverend." They were so funny.

Most of the men had never met a woman minister. I had the most adorable titles. "Miss Chaplain, Rev. Ma'am, Rev. Mother and Sister Reverend." When I opened the window shutter I saw his bright young smiling face! He was in a clean cell and his cough was gone. God had indeed answered our prayer! Although his security level had been heightened, it was just what he needed. The prison was also clean and bright. And the air was relatively clean too. I began to reevaluate what a blessing really is.

During a unit of CPE I had the opportunity to work with men and women in recovery for addictions. This was after I had found my husband's drugs. This is another journey that I would have never taken. I learned to love those struggling with drug and alcohol dependency. I had lived it. The one thing I knew was how much my husband struggled with his mood disorder. I often told him that whatever his problem was it was bigger than he and it had nothing to do with me. He needed psychiatric help. There was nothing left for me or those he tried to hold dear. For the first time, I understood the plight of a drug addict. I was proud of those I met in recovery. For whatever reasons, they were trying. Many were in recovery for the 2nd, 3rd and 4th time. At least they were trying. During those early years of my recuperation I also learned how hard it was to fill the emptiness inside.

I had no experience with drugs. I tried smoking a cigarette in junior high school. It did nothing for me. When drugs became popular in the early 70's, some of my schoolmates got hooked on heroin. I saw their promising futures destroyed.

Working in a hospital allows me to see the results of those who have abused their bodies for satan's scheme. I hated drugs. I hated drug dealers and I hated drug users. All that changed when I met Jesus inside the prison walls and when I married a man I loved with all my heart.

There were also times in my life where I couldn't work with women who did not take care of their children. I tried a stint with women in shelters around 1989. It was too hard. I had no sympathy or compassion for women who choose to be beaten. There was no room for weakness when it came to raising children. I know, I was one of those children who suffered under the hands of a weak mother. Somewhere in my depressed journey, I acquired some understanding of what it's like to be broken. Regardless of the situation, broken is broken. When I listened to the stories of the women whose drugs and alcohol took precedence over dignity, I really understood how they felt. Not only did I understand, but I had a bit of working knowledge to lend them. The one thing my breakdown afforded me was the opportunity to rebuild my life. It was really hard. Rebuilding my life was the most difficult thing I have ever had to do. There were times I did not think I was going to make it. I wanted to give up many times. Then I prayed and asked God to hold on to me tighter because the obstacles seemed so much larger than my resources and ability.

My profession gave me no advantage. It took a while before I could sit behind the chancel with the other clergy. In fact, if our senior pastor had not insisted that I join them in the pulpit, I would have remained in the pews. I had anxiety attacks for several months after I began sitting up there. One time I was so nervous that I began to say to myself, "Humpty Dumpty sat on a wall, Humpty Dumpty had a great fall. All the kings horses and all the king's men couldn't put Humpty together again. But God can." The one thing I knew without any doubts was that God is on my side. Whatever else has happened in my life, God has always been on my side.

Abiding under God's care began to transfer to others. Service is more than a sermon on Sunday morning and teaching Bible Study. I dearly love to teach the Bible but sometimes we must become the Bible. We must become God's hands and arms and legs. Service is also giving yourself to those who really need to know the hope that Christ offers. I was now able to give hope to women who did unforgivable things to their children. For the first time, I was no longer the hurting little girl who was afraid each time my mother gave in to her compulsion. I no longer had to hold my head down in my neighborhood. I remember seeing a man who had spent time at my mom's house. He was now old and on a cane. He looked at me with a smile. All I could think of was how he had invaded my space when I was a teenager. The drinking, the foul language, the lewdness. Either satan or me told me to smash his face! The headlines would read, "Able bodied Reverend takes cane of old man and smashes his face." Self-restraint is a good thing. For the first time in my life, those women were no longer my mother. I could hold my head up now. They were women whose circumstances had defeated them.

They were women who needed to know that in the midst of their plight, there was a God who loved them enough to die for them. They were valued. They could pull themselves up out of hell – they needed to take God's hand and hold on really tight. I held women who had never had a good hug. Both men and women wept when they learned that God wasn't holding anything against them. They had to learn how to forgive themselves. I am so thankful for my life with my husband. My husband robbed me of the joy and promise of marriage and his abuse caused me excruciating pain and humiliation. The experience also engrafted in me the precious love of God. Forgiveness became my way of life with him. Over and over, I prayed that God would give me his love for my husband. Loving my husband in my own strength almost destroyed me. A marriage from hell taught me things I never learned in seminary.

During my breakdown, my psychiatrist told me that until then I had only known the footsteps of Christ in theory. He assured me before I became well, I would experience what it might have been like for him. I was getting a glimpse of suffering. Those words were prophetic. He doesn't even remember saying them to me. I asked him days later to clarify what he meant. He said he did not know what I was talking about. He smiled and said perhaps someone else was speaking to me. The pain and suffering that I have experienced does hold a speck in comparison to the joy and the benefits of those experiences. I know souls are at stake. For the first time in my life, I know that I have been called by God to really help set the prisoners free. I obviously cannot reduce judicial sentences. My former husband has taught me that Christ's love can withstand the test of time and unpleasantness. My mind has not changed. I hate drugs. Calvary has taught me that its power is not limited. The destructive effects of addictive demonic spirits can be broken. My former husband has not changed but I am no longer a victim of his abuse and betrayal. Whether I liked it or not, his addiction was also my journey.

Encouragement

As I come to a close, the tears are beginning to flow. Dormant painful memories prompted me to tell my story. As I cried out to God (again) I realized that there are people who live with the pain of addiction and abuse each day. Loving a drug addict will not change his or her addiction. Many disciplines say that certain triggers will prompt a person to reevaluate their actions and how those actions are affecting those around them.

The trigger that caused me to write was seeing for myself how much I suffered and how far I have come. I suffered in silence for many years. I was too ashamed to tell. A few months ago I returned to school to earn a Doctorate of Ministry degree. I didn't know what was required to earn the degree. To my amazement, I had to discover something unique to me that would benefit others. The sovereignty of God has made it clear to me that I must tell the world what his grace and mercy has done for me. His grace and mercy is real. God wants to bless us. There has been one time that I was tempted to believe that God was not real. When my husband threw out my possessions, the pain was too much. I could not find God.

When I began to relive the humiliation and suffering I endured while we were married, I wanted to leave my church family. I could not relive that pain again. It would have been easy for me to go elsewhere. I decided to stay. I have hidden beneath shame too long. Shame and humiliation will not hold me captive any longer. God is strengthening me.

Some of you are not able to find God. Your pain has become too much. It is not God's best or his will for you to be degraded and abused for someone's sinful pleasure. My abuser also used crack-cocaine. Your abuser may have other vices. Mercy and grace is not unique to me. God is standing near. He is waiting for you to let him lead you out of your hell. You may have to go alone. God might change your abuser. The details are between God and you. It won't be easy nor will it be painless. Pain and fear should be the least of your concerns. You live in pain and fear each day. No two days are the same living with a drug addict. No two days are the same living with an abuser. You can't reason with an addictive demonic spirit. You can't reason with an abuser. He or she is bigger than you are. Addictive demonic spirits are bigger than you are. Abusers are not larger than God. Addictive demonic spirits are not larger than God. Abusers are not more powerful than God is. Addictive demonic spirits are not more powerful than God. Your abuser does not need your protection. God needs you to stop enabling your abuser to continue destroying the blessings he has stored up just for you and yours. Your blessings are waiting for you.

You have been wounded and broken. God wants to restore you. But first, he needs your help. You must help God bless you. Look in the mirror and see the wonderful person you are. Don't be afraid of the pain. It's there to remind you that you need God's help. Little by little, God will strengthen you. It is okay to cry, I highly recommend it. It is not okay to let addictive demonic spirits and/ or your abuser continue to destroy you and yours.

You are not alone. The pain and humiliation makes us feel as though we have been abandoned. God is with you. He will send others to help you walk your journey towards recovery. It will be difficult. Rebuilding always requires new tools. You've been torn down under the hand of your abuser. You must find new ways to appreciate yourself. You are worth it! Your name isn't bitch or whore. Don't buy into degradation. Hold up your head and walk tall. Remember, your abuser is strong because you have enabled him(her) to abuse you. Without your help, his (her) power will eventually dissipate. Use all of the resources at your disposal. Reach out into the greater community where you live. Take advantage of resources to rebuild your life. Don't tell your abuser your secrets. Abusers can't be trusted. They are not trustworthy.

You will rebuild, step by step. Don't expect anything from your abuser. He or she is incapable of loving or caring for you. You must learn a new appreciation for yourself. Make sure you are safe. Don't run away from your pain. I wanted to run too. Often we make a bigger mess for ourselves when we try to avoid or dull the pain. My former husband took away the only place I was safe from him. Then I realized that I am still safe. My mind wouldn't let me feel all the pain when I was still married to him. I could not bear it. I'm stronger now. You will get stronger too. Our painful emotions and memories need to heal. Sometimes your abuser will be in your presence. Please make sure you are safe. Then know God's healing balm is not limited or ineffective by your abuser's presence. If my colleague performs the wedding ceremony for my former husband, I expect that pain will greet me again. My colleague and his wife have shepherded me throughout this painful experience. With the help of my church family, I continue to heal and grow stronger. The many hugs and encouraging smiles have almost been worth the second go-round of pain. Whatever my colleague has comitted in his heart - if the pain greets me again, I will face it and live.

There will be many more New Year's Eves for me. I, like millions of others, felt there was nothing left to salvage. We trusted and were betrayed. God's mercy and blessings are new each day. God is faithful. God is taking the scraps of salvage and making me brand new. My former husband's betrayal, abuse and humiliation will not hold me captive. God is letting you and me know that it is time to go a little further. Trust God. He wants to make us whole again.

Dear Heavenly Father:

Thank you for hearing our cries. You are present in every abusive relationship. You see every insult, every slap and every tear. Sometimes we hurt so badly that we think you don't care. We aren't stupid, we were sincere. We hoped, we prayed and we did our best. Our abusers made a mockery of our devotion.

God please intervene. We are broken. Our abusers want to destroy us. Don't let them God. Protect us, fight for us. Help us to feel good about ourselves again. Help us know we are valued. Help us survive the hell we are in. You are greater than the addictive demonic spirits. You are greater than our abusers. Don't let them use their tactics against us. Fight them for us!

Send us help God. Strengthen us to receive the help you send. Help us bear the pain so we can talk about how we feel. Help us come from under our shame and despair. God help us to lift our heads again. Teach us how to fight back through prayer and affirming ourselves. Put angels around us to protect us and our children from our abuser's blows. Give us jobs and open doors so that we can get job training. Send us finances. Lord grant us whatever we need to rebuild our lives.

Father rid us of our abuser. We don't care how you choose to do it. Stand between us so that we can't keep hoping. God, help us to let go especially when fear tells us to hold on. Give us new direction and help us live again. Amen.

I am

a Survivor!

Journaling

Journaling

When I was recuperating from my breakdown, I learned how to express my feelings on paper. When I finished writing my story, I was amazed to see how far I have come! I continue to express my feelings on paper. The good days are worth celebrating too!

Journaling helped me cope when I thought I was alone. Pain and humiliation isolated me. Journaling helped relieve some of my pain. As I reflect and read years of expression, there were some days that I wrote only a few words. The pain was too much. There were also days that my former husband would give me a glimmer of kindness. I would write expressions of hope and thanksgiving.

I can also see when I began to break away from my co-dependent relationship with him. My thoughts became proactive. I was still hopeful but hope was rooted in my own choice to survive regardless of his demeanor towards me.

Use these few pages to begin your journey. Remember, your feelings are your own. Keep your journal in a safe place so that your privacy will be respected.

God is always with you, ask Him for direction when you can't find your way. Be encouraged, God will help you rebuild your life.

My Thoughts

You can have a better life. You are worth it! You are God's child! He will strengthen and help you. The Book of Philippians, Chapter 4, verse 13.

My Thoughts

God is totally committed to you. He loves you.
He wants to help you.
The Gospel According to John, Chapter 15, verse 13.

My Thoughts

You are made in the image and likeness of God.
The Book of Genesis, Chapter 1, verses 26-28.

My Thoughts

Rejoice! You are fearfully and wonderfully made!
The 139th Psalm

My Thoughts

*You are not alone. God wants to help
you stop hurting.
The Gospel According to Matthew,
Chapter 11, verses 28-30.*

My Thoughts

Lift up your head. Look to the Lord.
He will help you.
The 121st Psalm.

Page 109

My Thoughts

God will give you the faith to rebuild your life.
The Book of Hebrews, Chapter 12.

My Thoughts

*God is faithful and forgiving but He is also
a just God. Pray that He will protect you
from your enemy.
The 6th Psalm.*

My Thoughts

God doesn't condemn you.
He wants you to follow Him.
The Book of Romans, Chapter 8.
Page 112

My Thoughts

*When you are confused or don't know
what to do, "ask God." He will answer you.
The Book of James, Chapter 1.*

My Thoughts

Ask God to give you peaceful and sweet sleep.
It will make you feel better.
The 3rd Proverb, verse 24.

My Thoughts

*God will supply the resources you need to have
a good and productive life, "trust him."
The Book of Philippians, Chapter 4, verse 19.*

My Thoughts

Remember God is a spirit. When you can't find Him, He is still with you.
The 139th Psalm.
Page 116

My Thoughts

God will heal your broken heart.
He will give you more dreams! "Trust Him."
The 34th Psalm.

Page 117

My Thoughts

*Do not believe the negative things that
people are saying about you. Believe God.
The Book of Deuteronomy, Chapter 28, verse 13.*

My Thoughts

Learn a new way of life. Renew your mind so that you will know God's will for your life.
The Book of Romans, Chapter 12.

My Thoughts

*It is never too late to rebuild your life. God has
already made provisions for you, "go for it!"
The Book of Ephesians, Chapter 1.*

My Thoughts

Your children are a blessing regardless of your past experiences. Learn to love them the way God loves them.
The 127th Psalm.

My Thoughts

Be encouraged. God is able to do more than you can
ever imagine with your life!
The Book of Ephesians, Chapter 3, verse 20.

About the Author

The Reverend Versey A. Williams is an Itinerant Elder in the African Methodist Episcopal Church and a Board Certified Chaplain with the Association of Professional Chaplains.

She has a BA in the Management of Human Resources, MA in Educational Ministry and is presently a Doctorate of Ministry student at the Ecumenical Theological Seminary in Detroit, MI.

I pray that my journey with addiction has given you some new insight and hope for your future.